Talking Points

Discussion activities in the primary classroom

Lyn Dawes
with Paul Warwick

Routledge
Taylor & Francis Group

LONDON AND NEW YORK

First published 2012
by Routledge
2 Park Square, Milton Park, Abingdon, Oxon OX14 4RN

Simultaneously published in the USA and Canada
by Routledge
711 Third Avenue, New York, NY 10017

Routledge is an imprint of the Taylor & Francis Group, an informa business

British Library Cataloguing in Publication Data
A catalogue record for this book is available from the British Library

Library of Congress Cataloging-in-Publication Data
Dawes, Lyn.
  Talking points: discussion activities in the primary classroom/Lyn Dawes.
  p. cm.
  1. Communication in education. 2. Group work in education.
  3. Discussion—Study and teaching (Elementary)—Activity programs.
  4. Interpersonal communication—Study and teaching (Elementary)
  —Activity programs. I. Title.
  LB1033.5.D39 2011
  370.1′4—dc22
  2011014887

ISBN: 978-0-415-61458-0 (hbk)
ISBN: 978-0-415-61459-7 (pbk)
ISBN: 978-0-203-81869-5 (ebk)

Typeset in Bembo
by Florence Production Ltd, Stoodleigh, Devon

MIX
Paper from
responsible sources
FSC® C004839

Printed and bound in Great Britain by the MPG Books Group

This book is for
Anna McKay Mercer

Contents

5   Talking Points for lists   119

6   Talking Points for mathematics   129

Acknowledgements

I would like to acknowledge the contribution to this work made by my colleagues and students at Northampton University and the School of Education, Cambridge University. Their interest in and use of Talking Points has been an inspiration. In addition, many education professionals, teachers, students and children have spent time on the Talking Points resources, which has helped to clarify and create ideas. Special thanks to Linda Nicholls for her thoughtful suggestions for the stories and poems section. Thank you also to Bruce Roberts, James Hobbs, Charlotte Hiorns and Hamish Baxter, particularly for their patience and attention to detail. Arthur Pickering drew the charming illustrations – thank you, Arthur. And thank you to Neil for the informed comment and unwavering support throughout this book's production.

I am extremely grateful to have Paul Warwick's invaluable contribution to the science section.

Permissions

We are grateful to the following copyright holders for permission to reproduce their material:

Paul Muldoon, for 'Why Brownlee Left' from *Why Brownlee Left* (Faber and Faber, 1980), printed by kind permission of the publisher.

Ezra Pound, for 'In a Station of the Metro' from *Personae* (Faber and Faber, 2001), printed by permission of the publisher on behalf of Ezra Pound.

Robert Frost, for 'Spring Pools' from *Selected Poems* (Jonathan Cape, 2001), reprinted by permission of The Random House Group Ltd.

Jack Prelutsky, for 'The Invisible Beast' from The *Headless Horseman Rides Tonight: More Poems to Trouble Your Sleep* (HarperCollins Publishers, 1980). Text copyright © 1980 by Jack Prelutsky. Used by permission of HaperCollins Publishers.

Eleanor Farjeon, for 'The Quarrel' from *Silver, Sand and Snow* (Michael Joseph, 1951), reprinted by permission of David Higham Associates Ltd.

Louis MacNeice, for 'Snow' from *Collected Poems* (Faber and Faber, 2007), reprinted by permission of David Higham Associates Ltd.

Martin Honeysett, for 'Gorilla' from *Animal Nonsense Rhymes* (Egmont, 1984). Copyright © 1984 Martin Honeysett. Published by Egmont UK Ltd and used with permission.

Alfred Noyes, for 'The Highwayman', reprinted by permission of The Society of Authors as the Literary Representative of the Estate of Alfred Noyes.

David Scott, for 'Flanking Sheep in Mosedale' from *Selected Poems* (Bloodaxe Books, 1998), printed by permission of Bloodaxe Books.

Derek Mahon, for 'Bruce Ismay's Soliloquy' from *Poems 1962–1978* (Gallery Press, 1999), by kind permission of the author and The Gallery Press.

Pablo Picasso, for 'Weeping Woman', reproduced by permission of © Tate, London, 2011.

Vincent Van Gogh, for 'The Bedroom at Arles', Vincent Van Gogh: 'La chambre de Van Gogh à Arles', 1889 (RF 1959–2) Paris, musée d'Orsay and the RMN photo agency.

Every effort has been made to trace copyright holders, but in some instances this has not been possible. The publishers would like to apologise for any errors or omissions, and would appreciate being advised of any corrections that should be made to future editions of the book.

Introduction: What are Talking Points?

Talking Points are statements that encourage children to talk to one another about a topic, sharing what they know and understand. Talking Points support thoughtful discussion, analysis and reasoning, enabling children to consider everyone's ideas in detail. They help children to focus on the topic in hand, and to compare their point of view with that of others. Groups generate shared understanding or establish what it is that they do not know. They seek to reach an agreement; this might not be possible, and ultimately consensus is not important compared to the quality of the discussion and its impact on the child's mind. Children who understand the importance of talk for learning recognise a Talking Points discussion as a chance to articulate tentative ideas and consider a range of alternatives. During their group talk, individual children may well reach the limits of their understanding and realise that there is more to think about and learn.

ABOUT THE TALKING POINTS RESOURCES

Talking Points are thought-provoking statements. The statements might be right or wrong; they might suggest interesting or unusual ideas, or simply stimulate discussion that will elicit children's current thinking. Considering the statements helps children to reflect on different aspects of subjects. Talking Points are not questions. They require creative, analytical or evaluative thinking; they require children to provide reasons for what they say.

Talking Points are written in straightforward language with simple vocabulary. They are easy to read so that the ideas to discuss are immediately accessible. Children can concentrate their thinking on the subject under discussion.

TALKING POINTS DISCUSSION

Talking Points stimulate talk that ranges across many aspects of a topic, allowing children to take their time, listen, reflect and weigh up what they hear. Children in discussion share their personal experiences and understanding. They begin to see that some of their ideas are hypothetical and fluid, and can be affected by new evidence or insight. They recognise that classmates are a valuable resource for new thinking. They negotiate ideas by asking for and giving reasons for what is said. They learn to evaluate reasons and identify good reasons, and recognise the importance of basing decisions on sound evidence.

It is important to teach children how to take part in such educationally effective talk. Children may find talking about their own ideas quite difficult. They may not wish to share what they think, or to listen to others. They may not know that their discussion with classmates is an important way to learn. A feature of effective classrooms is the confident and measured talk between children engaged and motivated by learning from and with one another. Conversely, a feature of less effective classrooms is a heavy silence and children shielding their 'work' from one another, each pursuing a lonely course towards knowing better than anyone else – or not. Individual knowledge is not useful until creatively applied – that is, shared with others; learning and understanding have much less benefit to the individual if preserved as isolated achievements. Helping children to talk with others about what they know and understand helps minds to meet, friendships to form, and creativity to flourish.

PREPARING CHILDREN TO TALK TOGETHER IN A GROUP

Children may not recognise the crucial links between talking, thinking and learning. They need direct tuition to make this explicit.

Each child in a group – indeed, in a class – may have a different idea of what 'talk with your group' means. A group in which children think that sharing ideas is 'cheating', or that they must hurry to finish, gains little from discussion. Children who find it hard to listen, or those who think their own ideas are much more important than the ideas of others, need help if they are to gain access to a range of thinking. An overwhelming benefit of being part of a school class is that learning is social. But children must be helped to learn how to make the most of this. A profound understanding of how to relate to others in learning situations is not something children are born with! But it can readily be taught.

We have to prepare children for group work by teaching the talk skills and attitudes required for a good discussion. Indeed, these are life skills. Some children may already understand how to play an active and productive part in discussion. Such skills may be useless if others in the group lack awareness of the importance of talk for learning. Unless the whole class has worked together on their talk skills, there is no shared understanding that can lead to joint endeavour and effective collaboration.

Groups should be aware that they will be asked to contribute to a whole-class discussion after their talk together, about two things: the curricular or 'topic' content, and how well the group talked and worked together. They should be able to identify and remember incidents such as who asked a good question, changed their mind, encouraged someone else to talk, provided interesting ideas or information, and so on. In this way, they accumulate an understanding of the hidden but powerful ground rules that govern their talk with others. They begin to reflect on and become more aware of themselves as learners. Children should know that they will only be asked for positive comments on one another's group-talk skills. Difficulties within groups can be discussed separately, and evaluated as a basis for developing new talk strategies to try out.

TEACHING THE SKILLS CHILDREN NEED FOR EFFECTIVE GROUP DISCUSSION

How long you spend on this depends on your class. You can teach the following six ideas in six lessons, or you might want to take six months. Awareness of talk for learning and constant chances to practise discussion skills are invaluable, especially when coupled with direct input about talk skills, feedback on good practice, and a mix of evaluation of the effectiveness of group work and reminders about how groups work well throughout the school year.

Establishing **class ground rules for talk** is essential for effective group work. *(For more details of Talk Lessons, see further reading.)*

A summary of six essential Talk Lessons

1. Raising awareness of talk for learning and the value of the ideas of others

Discuss the use of talk for thinking and learning. Ask children how things can 'go wrong' when they are working together, and ask what can be done about it.

Show children that talk provides their best access to knowledge and understanding. Enable children to share their ideas with others. Ask the class to give examples of something new, interesting or helpful that they have heard.

2. Teaching children key words: 'exploratory talk' and 'interthinking'

Find out if children understand the characteristics of an effective discussion. Ensure that they know how to ask others to say what they think, to listen, to ask and give reasons, and to challenge with respect. Introduce the idea of exploratory talk for thinking and learning. Exploratory talk is educationally effective talk to which everyone in the group contributes fully. All ideas are backed up by reasons, which may be challenged and debated; the group seeks to reach agreement; and there is an atmosphere of tolerance, respect, interest and mutual support. Explain that, by thinking aloud – 'interthinking' – groups can do better than each person could alone.

3. Using key phrases to generate exploratory talk

Ask children to use key phrases during discussion, for example:

What do you think?

Why do you think that?

I agree because . . .

I disagree because . . .

. . . could you say more about . . .

. . . in summary, we could say . . .

Listen for developing uses of such phrases. Ask children to talk about their discussion, identifying benefits and considering problems. Ask for suggestions to help groups who are finding it difficult to discuss things properly.

4. Checking for listening, reflection and flexible thinking

Establish the idea of active listening as 'listening plus thinking'. Discuss what makes listening difficult, and ask children what listening strategies they use to contribute to a group discussion. Promote good listening by asking children to identify others who are good listeners; ask these children to say how and why they listen to others.

5. Exchanging and evaluating reasons

Discuss the importance of giving and listening to reasons. Familiarise children with simple strategies such as asking, 'Why do you think that?' and using 'Because . . .' Help them to see that there may be several reasons for points of view, some of which are contradictory. They need to know that they can evaluate reasons and make decisions about which reasons are 'better' because they are factually accurate, well argued or inspirational.

6. Shared ground rules for exploratory talk

Once the class has a raised awareness of talk for thinking and learning, they will have their own ideas about what makes a good discussion. Ask groups to suggest some straightforward rules that, if followed by everyone, would help to generate exploratory talk, and therefore help everyone to learn more readily. Collect a range of ideas. Generate a brief list and ensure that the class agree with them. Promote this list of ground rules for talk and use plenary sessions to check that groups focus on maintaining high quality discussion.

A Year 5 class generated these ground rules for talk based on their understanding of exploratory talk:

- We should all join in.
- It is important to ask why people say things.
- Listening to others and respecting ideas can help us to learn.
- We need to find out what everyone thinks and then try to agree.

The class applied these rules and used them to comment positively on one another's contributions during plenary discussion.

ORCHESTRATING WHOLE-CLASS TALK AFTER TALKING POINTS DISCUSSIONS

Children's ideas, brought out by the Talking Points, should be valued by sharing in subsequent whole-class talk. A group can be asked to explain their thinking on a particular point. Children can nominate a speaker who has something interesting to say on behalf of their group. Every child should be aware that, since they have all been party to the discussion, it is possible to ask any of them to contribute by name, thus avoiding 'hands up'. It is useful to ensure that contributions do not close down the discussion too suddenly. Keeping talk going helps children see how they can puzzle through ideas or bring further knowledge or understanding to bear. Some Talking Points have no definitive answer, and after discussion can be left open for future talk or research.

Each group's discussion is unique. It is never possible to share all ideas with the whole class. However, it is really important to orchestrate whole-class discussion based on Talking Points group work. It enables children to learn skills such as prioritising key points from group discussion, asking focused questions, and responding constructively to the ideas of others.

In addition, group talk is better focused when children know that, at some stage, they will be asked to contribute to a whole-class forum. For the teacher, whole-class talk is a terrific opportunity to assess children's understanding, taking note of misconceptions, expertise, and other ideas that will usefully inform future planning for the class or individuals.

A strong start to a whole-class discussion is to take a Talking Point that has raised uncertainty or interest, and ask one group to explain their thinking about it. Draw on what you have heard during group work, and ask particular children to repeat what they said. Everyone should have something to say, so 'hands up' is not necessary. Ask a child who has spoken to the whole class to choose who will contribute next. Contributions may need some summing up and rephrasing for clarity, but the discussion can proceed with children choosing who they think they want to hear from. Ask the class to choose girl-boy-girl and so on if you think this helpful or necessary.

Crucially, this part of the lesson is also a chance to comment on interesting ideas, clear thinking and reasoning. Ask groups to provide information about how well they worked together. Positive language is essential; children can give examples of group mates who asked good questions or who showed that they could change their mind. They can say who asked for contributions, gave interesting reasons, and so on; you can show the individuals mentioned how much you and the class value their contribution to the learning of others. Ask children if they heard the question 'What do you think?' Ask if everyone always agreed with what they heard, and how disagreements were negotiated. Ask for examples of good listening, and how it is possible to judge if others are listening. Ask children if they enjoyed talking together. Can they identify how new learning relates to this? Groups who have had problems can be asked to suggest what they can do about changing things. Other groups can be asked to suggest their ideas to help.

PLANNING FOR DISCUSSION

At what stage will group discussion be most valuable within your lesson? At the start, middle or end of a session – each has advantages. At the start, to take a sounding of current understanding; during group work, for children to learn from and with one another; at the end, to evaluate learning and share and consolidate newly conceived thoughts. Whatever you decide, because talk invariably takes longer than expected, it's important to ring-fence some time within your planning. This might well be the most important part of your lesson.

OUTCOMES OF TALKING POINTS DISCUSSION

Outcomes of discussion depend on your learning intentions. Discussion of ideas can become the basis for a range of curriculum-related work as individuals or groups:

- Note responses to the Talking Points, with reasons, in writing.
- Annotate a sketch or illustration.
- Make a storyboard or write an extra scene or verse.
- Carry out research or enquiry into their own questions.
- Make an information leaflet, fact cards, or a list.
- Create a quiz or question-and-answer resource.
- Plan a display.
- Create a PowerPoint presentation or web pages.
- Provide a role play, freeze frame or hot seat.
- Provide an oral or written report.
- Email children in their own or other schools.
- Write a story or a non-fiction text based on the topic.
- Write a review or evaluation of the topic or their discussion.

Discussion generates questions; sometimes it takes group talk for children to establish questions based on what they do not know. Children can research or investigate their own questions, with curiosity an intrinsic motivation.

Written work benefits from discussion. Children working individually or in their group to write about the discussion topic will have a range of resources to draw on. They can refer to one another for reminders or prompts. They have the confidence to be creative, knowing that they are not 'out on a limb' but have the strength of the group to call on. This does not mean that individuality is sacrificed. On the contrary, individual interpretation of group discussion is one of its most creative outcomes.

The main thing is to ensure that children can just get on with their discussion; but sometimes it can be useful to capture the essence of Talking Points discussions. Edited audio or video recordings, notes, sketches, or presentations offer the whole class invaluable insight into the thinking of groups.

CREATING YOUR OWN TALKING POINTS

You can create Talking Points that match a topic with the level of your children's understanding. First, think of a list of factual information or opinions about a topic that you will be teaching. Find a relevant resource – a poem, story, or picture. Sometimes ideas will come from things you have heard the children say.

Now turn your starting facts or opinions into about ten slightly puzzling ideas that will get the children talking. It can help to think of these statements as having an answer 'true, false, or unsure'. Avoid questions – this is important. Questions need a definite answer. Talking Points put the children in the position of having to justify their ideas and articulate their thinking rather than come up with an answer. In effect, the children position Talking Points as a 'voice', the voice of someone they can have a real argument with, ranging themselves as a group on one side of the discussion and the anonymous (and sometimes exasperating) Talking Points voice on the other.

Express your Talking Points simply and concisely in a numbered list. The numbers are important for quick reference during plenary discussion. Language used should be straightforward so that the statements are easily read. In effect, the reading age of the children should be two years or so higher than the reading they will need to share a Talking Point. Talk groups should be constituted so that children who cannot read fluently are not at any disadvantage since reading ability is not relevant for thinking, talking and learning.

Talking Points can be printed or displayed on screen. Children should know that they do not write answers, but concentrate on their talk with others.

How many Talking Points to write? This is a difficulty that your professional understanding of your class can resolve. Initially, you may need to provide a list of Talking Points because children who are still developing discussion skills cannot engage with one idea for very long, but tend to decide that they have said enough after the briefest of exchanges. As your class learn how to ask probing questions, to bring in related information and ideas, and to discuss and analyse reasons, fewer Talking Points are necessary. As a teacher, I am always worried by groups who rush through the points with superficial engagement and abbreviated talk, and then declare they are finished. 'What shall we do now?' they ask. It is important to ensure that there is time enough for other discussions that are going on around the room to continue. My two strategies to ensure there is space and time for real talk to take place are first to write a whole string of Talking Points, too many for most groups to tackle; and second to think of an extension activity to complete the Talking Points resource. This can involve the group using their ideas to create something or do further work together. Those who rush their discussion (a stage on the way to learning how to think aloud with others) are productively occupied while others continue to talk. However, you may feel that a long list of Talking Points encourages superficial engagement and looks a bit daunting. I think that you need to negotiate this with your class. Do they prefer to have lots to talk about, choosing to move on if discussion stalls on a particular point? Do they prefer to have just three or four Talking Points and really try to concentrate on these?

Examples of extension activities can be found at the end of the Talking Points resources.

Groups who feel that they have said enough can be asked to prepare to talk about the quality of their group discussion, thinking of examples of active listening, interthinking, and asking and giving reasons, or evaluating reasons; or identifying problems with talk, and suggesting strategies to improve things.

BUILDING UP VOCABULARY

(a) Include key words in the Talking Points statements, in an accessible context.

(b) Highlight three or four key words and ask children to make sure that they use them during their discussion. For example, talking about magnets, you might first provide the words **poles**, **repel**, **attract**, **field**, **force**.

(c) Ask groups to write their own Talking Point using one or more of the key vocabulary words for the topic.

(d) Use the words you want children to use, during your plenary discussion with them.

TEACHING CHILDREN TO CREATE TALKING POINTS

You can teach children how to make up Talking Points.

1   Provide the class with a stimulus that relates to your topic – for example, a historical artefact, a model, toy or picture; a machine, utensil, animal or plant; a poem, a story, a drawing or cartoon; a map or a book.

2   Provide a context for discussion. Ask the children to talk together in their groups to decide on three things that they know about the topic, and **write down these three ideas**. Next, ask the groups to talk together to think of three things that they do not know about the resource, and **write down three questions** they would like to ask. Collect the written ideas and questions.

Alternatively, if looking for opinions rather than knowledge, ask children to discuss three things they **like** or **admire** about the resource, and three things they **dislike**, both with reasons. They can also discuss **who** they think would like something that they do not.

Another way to elicit a range of ideas is to provide a list of question starters, and ask children to think about your resource and discuss a response to each:

is it . . .

who . . .

why . . .

where . . .

what . . .

when . . .

what if . . .

what does it . . .

can we . . .

what story . . .

can we think of similar . . .

do you remember . . .

3   Using the statements and questions provided by the groups, generate a list of ten Talking Points that you think will stimulate further thinking and help children to consider their own ideas and those of others. You can also use the questions as starters for further practical enquiry or research.

USING THE TALKING POINTS IN THIS BOOK

The Talking Points can be photocopied. Some have a reminder about the focus on high-quality talk. All require children to know how to engage one another in exploratory talk.

Many of the Talking Points have statements that could be thought of as true or false, and, in this case, reasons are necessary for answers. An answer of 'unsure' is always valuable. It can reflect a group's uncertainty once they have considered all the information and opinions they can offer. It indicates a readiness to learn.

Some of the mathematics resources comprise statements that are all accurate. In this case, the group will talk together to show how they can justify the statement, to provide examples, and to ensure that everyone agrees with the reasoning they will offer to the whole class. Some of the Talking Points are lists. The discussion here is to do with considering which items are appropriate to stay on the list and which are not; and to generate new ideas to add to the list. For some of the history Talking Points, the discussion is to do with talking about a particular point of view in the light of our perspective on the past, and generating a role-play as a response.

I would be delighted to hear of your classroom talk or to see Talking Points that you or your class have created, and I hope you and the children really enjoy talking about their ideas.

Talking Points
for science

The Talking Points in this section are designed to elicit a range of ideas about the natural world. Children's everyday observations of how the world works lead them to generate their own informal explanations about things. They may never articulate these ideas but hold them to be 'true' because they seem to account for what is observed. Some such everyday ideas are tenuous and easily changed; others are much more deeply rooted. It is not unusual for any of us to hold on to our own explanations for things even though we can understand a more scientific conception of the world.

Responses to these Talking Points can include:

■ we agree with this, because . . .

■ we disagree with this, because . . .

■ we are unsure but think that . . .

■ we have different points of view about this, which are . . .

Each set of Talking Points concludes with a Thinking Together activity in which children share their ideas to draw, write, create or record some aspect of the theme.

You may wish to provide the whole list of Talking Points, to put up two or three for more focused discussion, or to allocate different points to different groups. They can be used to start a lesson, as part of group work within a lesson, or as part of a plenary or revision session. After group discussion, it is important to orchestrate a whole-class discussion in which a range of views are shared and considered.

These science Talking Points are accompanied by information in the form of *teacher's notes*, contributed by Paul Warwick of the faculty of Education at the University of Cambridge. These are for use in planning and teaching or with groups *after* their discussion. **Children should not be provided with copies of the notes during their group talk**, as reading and looking for 'right answers' hampers effective discussion.

TALKING POINTS: SMALL CREATURES

Talking Points

What does your group think of these ideas?

1 All creepy crawlies are insects.

2 Insects all eat plants.

3 Spiders and insects are the same thing.

4 Woodlice have live babies; they do not lay eggs.

5 The woodlouse has a hard outside shell.

6 The woodlouse has more legs than a spider.

7 Woodlice move at different speeds.

8 Woodlice have more in common with lobsters than with spiders.

9 Snails are both male and female.

10 Slugs are snails that are in between one shell and the next size up.

11 There is more than one sort of worm.

12 Ladybirds lay eggs and tiny ladybirds hatch out in summer.

13 Insects have six legs, so a caterpillar is not an insect.

14 Butterflies have scales on their wings.

15 Moths find their way by using light and scent.

16 Beetles all have hard wing cases.

17 Dragonflies are carnivores.

18 Composting is helped by worms.

19 In Victorian times, there were 100 times more butterflies than now.

20 Some insects use camouflage to protect themselves.

THINKING TOGETHER

Talk with your group to design and draw a plant that can catch insects. Say why it would get its food this way.

14

Information: Small creatures

Many small creatures are **invertebrates**. The term 'invertebrate' refers to about 30 groups of animals, all of which have no backbone or internal skeleton. 90 per cent of all creatures on the planet are invertebrates and there are over 250,000 different kinds of invertebrates in Britain. Many have soft bodies; some have a thin, strong **exoskeleton** – such as beetles.

Butterflies, moths and beetles are all **insects**, the most diverse of all animal groups. They have six legs and three body parts – head, **thorax** and **abdomen**. Some insects are **herbivores** and eat plants while others, such as dragonflies, are **carnivores**. Ladybirds are a type of beetle – an insect with a hard exoskeleton and hard wing cases. They lay eggs, which hatch into larvae that eat greenfly voraciously. Butterflies and moths can be distinguished by their **antennae**; those of the moth are pointed (male) or like fronds (female), while butterfly antennae are clubbed. Both butterflies and moths have good eyesight and the ability to follow scent. They are suffering because of **habitat** loss; in Victorian times, there were at least 100 times more butterflies than there are now.

Caterpillars are the immature stage of certain kinds of insects (most notably butterflies and moths) and undergo **metamorphosis** to become the adult stage. A caterpillar has a head, three pairs of true legs on the thoracic segments and a segmented abdomen.

Spiders are **arachnids** and have a tough external covering and jointed legs. Spiders have two body parts and eight legs, each with eight joints. The weight of insects eaten by spiders each year exceeds the weight of the human population of the world. Woodlice are **crustaceans** (related to lobsters and crabs). Females keep their eggs underneath their bodies until they hatch, then seem to 'give birth' to live young. The woodlouse has a hard outside carapace. As a woodlouse grows the 'shell' falls off and it grows a new, bigger, one. Woodlice have fourteen legs and their speed of movement depends on the situation in which they find themselves (rather like us!).

Snails and slugs are **gastropod** molluscs – gastro is for stomach and pod is for foot, so they are 'belly-footed' animals. Though descended from snails, slugs are a different species, rather than simply snails without shells. There are many types of **worm**. Worms sift earth and organic material, improving soil drainage and texture – they convert compost to soil. Earthworms have segmented bodies and they are able to replace damaged tail-end segments, while other types of worm are un-segmented. Charles Darwin spent 39 years studying the humble earthworm, so they are worthy of our attention.

TALKING POINTS: MICRO-ORGANISMS

Talking Points

True, false, or unsure? *Talk together* **to decide on your group's answer to these ideas, making your reasons clear.**

1 Micro-organisms are the same thing as germs.

2 There are germs all around us.

3 We always get ill when we catch a germ.

4 We can explain exactly what a virus is (practise trying!).

5 A bacteria and a virus are the same thing.

6 You can only catch germs through the air.

7 There is nothing you can do to stop germs spreading.

8 We don't have any germs!

9 Antibiotics are medicines that kill bacteria and viruses.

10 Bacteria can be useful: we can think of some examples.

11 Fungi can be useful: we can think of some examples.

12 Some of our food contains bacteria and it tastes nice.

13 It is best to live in a totally germ-free environment.

14 If you wash your hands for less than 10–20 seconds, it doesn't work.

THINKING TOGETHER

Talk with your group to draw or list examples of all the ways we can store food to slow down growth of bacteria and fungi.

Information: Micro-organisms

Micro-organisms (or **microbes**) are organisms that are too small to see without a powerful microscope; bacteria are about 1,000th of a millimetre across. Micro-organisms may be bacteria, fungi, algae, protozoa or viruses.

Algae are close relatives of plants; they can photosynthesise and have a nucleus. **Protozoa** are single-celled organisms that get their food from the surrounding environment – either freshwater, seas or the soil.

Bacteria are single-celled organisms without a nucleus. They are usually shaped like a sphere, rod or spiral, and have a tail (**flagellum**) that enables movement. They were the first form of life on Earth and are everywhere, living in a huge range of environments and temperatures. Most are very useful to us – producing oxygen, helping us to digest food and helping plants to extract nitrogen from the soil. We use them in the manufacturing of cheese and yogurt, and for cleaning water in sewage plants.

Fungi, which were once thought to be plants, now have their own **kingdom** in the classification of organisms. Some of the larger fungi are mushrooms and toadstools. Microbial fungi can be as beneficial; for example, **yeast** is a single-celled fungus, used to make bread rise and to produce the alcohol in beer by fermentation. **Penicillin** is an **antibiotic** made from a fungus. Fungi help dead leaves break down to become soil. Also, fungi make the blue veins in some cheeses.

Viruses are the smallest type of microbe and do not fit within the classification of five kingdoms of living things. Some scientists don't consider viruses to be alive; just active when in a living cell and inactive when not inside one. They are bundles of genetic code (**DNA** or **RNA**) in a **protein** shell. Viruses can cause disease in humans, animals or plants. Common diseases caused by viruses include influenza and chicken pox.

Germ is a term used to describe a range of micro-organisms – bacteria, viruses, protozoa and fungi – that cause us harm or bring disease. Most environments contain bacteria or viruses that we would describe as germs. It is difficult to create and maintain a sterile (germ-free) environment, but simple procedures such as hand washing can significantly reduce germs. It is not sensible to live in a totally germ-free environment because contact with germs helps us to develop and maintain immunity to them.

The most common ways in which germs are transferred are through water droplets (coughing and sneezing) and through physical contact. But our bodies have more or less effective **immune systems** that defend us by working to stop the number of 'bad microbes' multiplying and spreading. So we don't always get ill when germs are transferred to us. If you do come into contact with germs, you might be given antibiotics. Antibiotic means 'against life', and antibiotic medicines can only deal with bacteria. Your doctor won't give you antibiotics for a viral infection because viruses, being fragments of cells, are not truly 'alive' and so are unaffected by such medicines.

TALKING POINTS: THE AIR AND BREATHING

Talking Points

What do you think? Why? Can your group agree?

1   Air is made of lots of invisible gases.

2   The air is mainly oxygen.

3   We only breathe in oxygen.

4   We breathe out carbon dioxide.

5   Carbon dioxide is a dangerous gas.

6   Carbon dioxide causes the greenhouse effect, which is bad for the Earth.

7   Our lungs are designed to hold a lot of air.

8   Breathing is caused by muscles, not lungs.

9   Lungs are damp inside.

10 When we breathe in, air is pumped into the blood.

11 We lose water to the air by breathing out.

12 Exercise helps to develop healthy lungs.

13 In the lungs, oxygen moves from the air into red blood cells.

14 Air that is polluted by smoke can damage the lungs.

15 When you have a bad cough, your lungs are infected with a disease.

THINKING TOGETHER

Talk together to draw and label a diagram explaining why you breathe more quickly when you have been running about.

Information: The air and breathing

The air is made of invisible gases; approximately 80 per cent **nitrogen**, 19 per cent **oxygen**, and 1 per cent a mix of **carbon dioxide**, **carbon monoxide**, **helium**, **neon**, **argon** and other **trace gases**. We breathe in air, but our bodies only use the oxygen from it, and only absorb this into the bloodstream. We breathe out air that has a slightly raised carbon dioxide level because this is a waste product of body **metabolism**, and breathing enables us to get rid of it.

Carbon dioxide at its usual concentration of about 0.03 per cent in air is crucial for life on earth. It is the source of the carbon that plants need for photosynthesis. But, in high concentrations, carbon dioxide is lethal for humans and other animals. It is also one of the **greenhouse gases** that contributes towards excessive **global warming**. The **greenhouse effect** involves gases absorbing heat energy radiated from the Earth, eventually making the overall temperature of the atmosphere higher than it would otherwise have been. This mechanism is essential for life on Earth . . . but a greenhouse effect enhanced by unusually high concentrations of carbon dioxide, water vapour and other gases creates an unstable Earth environment. Scientific evidence now indicates that human activity has produced an enhanced greenhouse effect in relatively few decades. This is creating a level of global warming and is predicted to have dramatic effects on the Earth's climate. The term 'global warming' implies a pleasant sunnier climate; however, a more accurate term is 'climate chaos'. We may be already witnessing extreme weather events such as floods or droughts, un-seasonal snow or high temperatures.

In the lungs, we each have about 700 million small air sacs called **alveoli**. On average, we inhale and exhale about 22,000 times a day. This varies with age and exercise. **Lung capacity** can reach six litres. During breathing, muscles move the ribs and the **diaphragm**, so making air move in and out of the lungs. Oxygen entering the lungs dissolves on the damp lining of the alveoli and, in solution, is absorbed into red blood corpuscles. We lose water to the air when we breathe out.

During breathing, oxygen moves from the air into red blood cells and carbon dioxide moves out into the air; this is known as **gas exchange**. Air that is polluted by smoke or other substances can damage the lungs. The cilia, protective hairs that line the airways, are paralysed by some chemicals found in smoke and are unable to help keep the lung surfaces clear. Alveoli become less 'stretchy'; an accumulation of chemicals such as tar creates the conditions for cells to become cancerous, and smoke can also encourage the bacteria that cause pneumonia and other infections. Problems with lungs may be indicated by a cough; coughs have many causes and a doctor should be consulted.

TALKING POINTS: IN THE GARDEN

Talking Points

Talk together to decide if you agree with these ideas. What are your reasons?

1 Gardens are boring; only old people do gardening.

2 Gardens are best if they are mainly grass for football.

3 Gardens always belong to houses – we can't share them.

4 Lots of gardens have been made into parking spaces.

5 Gardens are alive.

6 Gardens should be kept free of weeds, and very neat and tidy.

7 We can name six birds that might visit a garden (practise it!).

8 We can name three wild mammals that visit gardens.

9 We can name three insects that might be in a garden.

10 Spiders are horrible and no one likes them.

11 Hedgehogs eat slugs and snails, so gardeners like them.

12 Slug pellets kill slugs, so they are good.

13 Feeding birds is bad because dropped food attracts rats.

14 Nettles are no good for anything and should all be chopped down.

15 Compost is disgusting!

THINKING TOGETHER

Think together to draw and label a garden that is wildlife-friendly.

Information: In the garden

Gardening has been a popular activity in the UK for over a century, with particular interest in gardening for **food crops** during World War II. Though the majority of gardeners are older (the average age of a 'keen gardener' in 2010 was 54), many younger people enjoy gardening. Roads and car parks have meant that some gardens have been lost. In addition, houses are being built with small gardens unsuitable for growing food. Some people without gardens can rent allotments. An allotment is an area of land usually owned by a Local Authority. The first mention of allotments appears in the late 1500s. Under Elizabeth I, common lands used for growing food and keeping animals began to be enclosed, dispossessing the poor who then had no means to feed themselves. In compensation, 'allotments' of land were attached to tenant cottages.

Gardeners are both helped and hindered by the presence of animals. The potential benefits of worms and spiders are mentioned in the section of this book on small creatures. Less beneficial are slugs and snails, which damage garden crops. They eat with a **radula**, a muscular structure coated by thousands of teeth that rasp against the food plant, scraping away particles. This is extremely effective in devastating plant collections! So it's little wonder that gardeners like animals that eat slugs and snails, such as toads, hedgehogs (though snails and slugs are only about 5 per cent of a hedgehog's diet) and thrushes (which eat snails when the ground is baked or frozen and they can't find worms). Other creatures also help the gardener; for example, blue tits are fond of aphids and caterpillars, ladybirds devour greenfly, and bats consume high numbers of insects on the wing each night and are a main predator of mosquitoes and midges.

Gardeners need to be quite careful when using poisonous chemicals. Slug pellets are pieces of cereal soaked in **metaldehyde**. The cereal acts as bait, attracting the slug and then poisoning it. Metaldehyde is classed as 'moderately hazardous' by the World Health Organisation. This means that, although it is effective against slugs, it poses a risk to anything else that eats it – including pets, wildlife and children. Luckily, many gardeners see the benefits of 'organic gardening' or 'gardening for wildlife'. They do not use chemicals in their gardens and they avoid creating extremely neat gardens. There is space for wild flowers such as nettles to grow, providing food for the caterpillars of several butterfly species such as the red admiral, peacock, small tortoiseshell and comma. 'Weed' is a term meaning a wild flower unwanted where it is growing, but luckily many gardeners welcome wild flowers. Composting is an important part of organic gardening, since a compost heap not only prevents many millions of tons of material ending up in landfill sites, but breaks down organic material to enable **nitrogen-rich compost** to be returned to the garden soil.

TALKING POINTS: PROBLEMS FOR THE EARTH

Talking Points

What does your group know or understand about these topics? Are the ideas here true, or false, or are you unsure?

1   The greenhouse effect has always affected conditions on Earth.

2   Global warming is good because it's going to make our climate in the UK similar to living near the Mediterranean.

3   In terms of the universe, the human race is not necessary and it will not matter if it becomes extinct.

4   It is pointless for us to try to 'be green' because there is so much pollution in countries such as China and the USA – that is what really makes the difference.

5   Climate change is for politicians, businesspeople and newspapers. We cannot make any difference ourselves.

6   Rich people cause most pollution and damage to the Earth.

7   We should not be made to feel worried about the future of the planet. Things will turn out as they are meant to be.

THINKING TOGETHER

Excessive global warming is expected to cause the sea level to rise; more extreme weather events; deserts to spread; poor harvests of food crops and the extinction of many plants and animals.

Talk together about the two sentences below. What does your group think? Draw an illustration that shows the things you personally do to help create less pollution or to 'be green'. Say how your class or school could use your ideas to 'be green'.

1   Many species are unnecessary and will not be a loss to the planet.

2   The earth has always changed. We humans can control our own environment whatever the weather, so we will be fine.

Information: Problems for the Earth

The '**greenhouse effect**' describes how **radiant energy** from the Earth is absorbed by greenhouse gases (such as **carbon dioxide** and **water vapour**), eventually making the overall temperature of the atmosphere higher than it would otherwise have been. This mechanism is essential for life on Earth . . . but an *enhanced* greenhouse effect creates an unstable Earth environment. Much scientific evidence now indicates that human activity has produced an enhanced greenhouse effect in relatively few decades, creating a level of **global warming** that is predicted to have dramatic effects on the Earth's **climate**.

The recorded effects of the current warming of the Earth's atmosphere include ice melting worldwide, with a consequent rise in global sea levels. Precipitation (rainfall and snowfall) has increased across the globe. There have been some dramatic effects on animal and plant populations, such as the decline of the Adélie penguins in Antarctica, where numbers have fallen from 32,000 breeding pairs to 11,000 in 30 years. But it is difficult to say with precision how the weather in a particular part of the world will be changed by changes in the Earth's climate associated with global warming.

Large industrialised nations and better-off people tend to produce more waste, contributing both to global warming and environmental degradation. But we can each take positive action to reduce pollution, waste, and energy and water use. For example, for every ton of paper that is recycled, 7,000 gallons of water, 380 gallons of oil and enough electricity to power an average house for six months are saved. So it's worth considering what each of us might do.

Societies and governments can choose whether to adopt 'clean' technologies rather than those that contribute excessively to global warming and the pollution of the environment. There are technologies that can make a difference; for example, devices that capture solar energy and convert it to electricity. But we cannot just rely on technology. And if humans disappear, will it make a difference? Extinctions are part of the normal evolutionary process and it is estimated that over 99 per cent of all species that have ever lived are now extinct. The current degrading of the world environment may make it more likely that humans join that list. This will mean nothing in evolutionary terms, but would be rather a shame for us! People are a resilient, inventive and interesting life form. We will not be missed by the universe in general; but the loss of life on Earth would be a tremendous shame and really is unnecessary. We can hope that the wish to survive and to pass the chance for life on to future generations will enable individuals and societies to act in ways that help, rather than destroy, the environment. Each of us can play our part. There were over 6 billion people on earth in 2000 and there may be 9 billion by 2050 – so everyone needs to help.

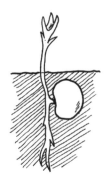

TALKING POINTS: SEEDS

Talking Points

What do you know about seeds? Share your ideas.

1   Seeds are empty until they start to grow.

2   Seeds have to be in soil to grow.

3   Seeds have everything they need to grow inside them.

4   Seeds are completely waterproof.

5   Seeds need it to be spring before they will grow.

6   Some seeds have a food store in them, for the new young plant.

7   Seeds will not grow if it is light.

8   Bigger seeds grow bigger plants.

9   We can eat a lot of types of seeds.

10   Many types of birds live on seeds.

11   Seeds are a good way for plants to get through the winter.

12   Some plants can make new plants without having seeds.

13   Germination means 'seeds sprouting'.

14   There is a difference between what seeds need to germinate and what young plants need to grow and develop.

THINKING TOGETHER

Imagine that you are sending some seeds to a class of younger children. Design the packet. Draw some seeds. Provide a clear description to show the things your seeds need to start them growing. Make sure you say what should not happen to the seeds; for example, they should not be cooked!

Information: Seeds

Seeds have a basic structure of a protective **seed coat** or hull, a **food source** and the **embryo** of a new plant. The seed coat is tough and protects the embryo and food source, so that seeds can last over harsh winter conditions, or through a drought. Some seed coats such as ash, sycamore and yew have flattened or papery extensions to the seed coat, which help the seeds to float on the air and **disperse** well. The seed coat may have a 'scar' where the seed was held in the parent plant. Seeds are not completely waterproof; there is a small hole to allow water in so that, in favourable conditions, enough water is absorbed to begin the processes that will lead to **germination**.

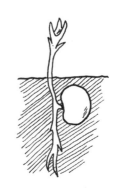

The food source within a seed usually contains starch, because this is insoluble, but may also contain protein and oils. The embryo, or 'germ', may contain protein. Some seeds such as beans and peas are divided into two cotyledons; others have a single **cotyledon**. Plants are classified by the number of cotyledons their seeds have. Monocotyledons are plants such as orchids and all the different sorts of grasses. Dicotyledons include flowering plants.

The embryo plant usually has a **plumule** or shoot, and a **radicle** or root. The radicle will grow first when water is available, developing a large surface area of root hairs to absorb as much water as possible. **Enzymes** convert the food store into products that the new plant can use for growth. The food store allows the radicle and plumule to grow until the new leaves develop and unfold and are able to synthesise sugars and other organic chemicals. The plant does not usually need light until the food store is used up – light is not a condition for germination. Germinated seeds that are kept in the dark grow long, yellowing and stringy shoots – they are **etiolated** – as they 'search' for a light source. The tip of the shoot is sensitive to light and grows towards light.

Seeds need different conditions for germination, depending on the plant. Some need a period of drought, cold, or even fire, before they are ready to begin growing. Usually, seeds need water, air and some warmth to germinate. Seeds vary in size from orchids, which are like fine dust, to large Maldive Coconuts, which can weigh up to 42 kg.

TALKING POINTS: FORCE

Talking Points

Are these true, false, or is your group unsure?

1   A small object can fall to the ground at the same speed as a large object.

2   Things stop when they run out of force.

3   A large ship takes a long time to stop because there is little friction between its hull and the water.

4   A marble has a gravitational field and attracts other objects.

5   There is no gravity above the Earth's atmosphere.

6   The weight of an object measures how much stuff it's made up of.

7   A larger object always has more air resistance.

8   A falling parachute pulled down by gravity is pushed up by air resistance.

9   You can reduce pressure by spreading weight out over a larger area.

10   The air is too light to be affected by the Earth's gravity.

11   The weight of water in a glass creates pressure, which pushes equally in all directions, including upwards.

12   Steel ships float because they have air in them.

THINKING TOGETHER

Think together to draw a picture of the forces involved in:

■ a game of football, tennis, netball or cricket

■ swimming, walking, ice hockey

■ playing a musical instrument such as a piano, guitar or recorder

■ the equipment at a play park or funfair, and

■ riding a bike or going out on roller blades.

Information: Force

Forces are pushes or pulls. We can feel the effect of a **contact force** as someone pushes against us, or a **non-contact force** as gravity pulls us back to the ground if we jump upwards. Pressure is the force acting on each unit area of a surface. If you stand on a surface, the force of your weight acts as pressure through the surface area of your shoes.

Gravitational force occurs as a consequence of objects having **mass**. Objects with mass exert a **gravitational field** on other objects. However, gravity is rather a weak force. So, it is only when objects get very big indeed that their gravitational field has a really significant effect. The correct way of expressing this is that the **gravitational force of attraction** between two objects is proportional to their masses. Larger objects pull with more force.

The Moon and Earth are attracted to one another by their gravitational fields, and both are influenced by the huge gravitational field of the Sun. The interaction between the objects in the solar system influences where they are and how they move. The gases of our atmosphere are held to the Earth by gravity.

The **mass** of an object is the amount of 'stuff' it's made from, measured in kilograms. Weight is a measure of the gravitational force pulling anything with mass to the Earth. Weight is measured in **Newtons**. If you travel into space you still have the same mass – the amount of stuff you're made from – but your weight decreases as you move further away from the gravitational influence of the Earth. If you were to travel to Mars, you'd find yourself on a world that has a diameter only half of that of the Earth, with only 10 per cent of its mass. Because of its low mass, the gravity on Mars is only 38 per cent of the gravity on Earth; if you weigh 100 kg on Earth, you would weigh 38 kg on Mars. So, travel to Mars if you want to lose weight!

On Earth, objects fall to the ground as a result of the gravitational attraction between the object and the Earth. The Italian scientist Galileo Galilei dropped two different weights from Pisa's leaning tower and demonstrated that they landed at the same time. Galileo made sure that he took air resistance into account. He knew that differently shaped objects with the same mass would move through the air differently – which we can see by dropping a piece of paper flat or 'edge first'. **Air resistance** is a **frictional force** that acts to oppose motion, and the larger the surface area the greater the air resistance on an object.

Where there is no air at all, as on the moon, all objects fall at the same rate. There is a famous film clip showing Apollo 15 Commander David Scott performing a live demonstration of this on the moon in 1971. He held out a geological hammer and a feather and dropped them at the same time - with no air resistance, the feather fell to the moon's surface at the same rate as the hammer. The moon has no air because it is not massive enough to generate the amount of gravity needed to hold an atmosphere.

TALKING POINTS: MAGNETISM

Talking Points

Are these points true or false? Use exploratory talk to interthink. Share your reasons. Be ready to explain.

1   Magnets have poles. The north pole of a magnet points north.

2   The earth is a very large magnet.

3   Some metals are attracted to magnets – not all. We can say which are.

4   Magnetism is a force. We can name some other forces.

5   Magnetism is strongest near the ends of magnets.

6   Magnets are rectangles so that the magnetism can run to each end.

7   Magnets always point in the same direction if free to move.

8   You can make magnetism from electricity, and electricity from magnetism.

9   Magnets don't work under water.

10 Magnets attract each other and repel each other.

11 We get the word magnet from the metal magnesium.

12 A compass needle is a magnet that turns as the Earth turns.

13 If you cut a magnet in half, you get two magnets.

14 We can say why a mobile phone picks up some 1 pence pieces.

THINKING TOGETHER

Think together to draw a compass with eight points. Label it to explain how a compass works. Use a plotting compass to plot the magnetic field of a bar or horseshoe magnet.

Information: Magnetism

Greek stories have different accounts about the name
'magnet'; that it derives from a place in Greece called
Magnesia, or that a shepherd named Magnes was the first to
discover a **lodestone** (a natural magnet) when his crook,
which had an iron tip, was pulled towards a stone.

Magnetism is a **non-contact force** that is evident in the
ferro-magnetic metals iron, cobalt or nickel, and their alloys,
such as steel. Such materials can become magnets through contact with a **magnetic
field** or electrical current. The atoms of all objects contain electrons and these carry an
infinitesimally small electrical charge. When electrons move, as they do all the time, then
their electrical charges move and this generates a tiny magnetic field. When this happens
in most objects, the magnetic fields from the electrons are all acting in different
directions; but in ferro-magnetic metals, the electrons can all face in the same direction,
creating a magnetic field around the whole object. This magnetic field can work through
non-magnetic materials, through water, even through a vacuum, but magnetism
becomes increasingly weak through layers of other magnetic material.

Magnetism is a mysterious force, since what a magnetic field actually is remains
something of a mystery. We do know that it flows from one end of a magnet to the
other. By convention, we call one end the **N** or **north-seeking pole** and the other the
S or **south-seeking pole**. The north pole of a magnet held in a way that allows
movement, 'seeks' the north magnetic pole of the Earth. The Earth's own magnetic field
is becoming weaker; at the present rate, it will be gone in a thousand years. This may be
related to the planet preparing to swap its north and south magnetic poles around, as it
has done many times before during Earth's history.

The rule for magnets is '**like poles repel, unlike poles attract**'. A freely suspended
magnet will come to rest with its N-seeking pole facing northwards, and vice-versa, and
this is used in a plotting compass. The poles of a magnet are areas that produce a
stronger force of attraction than other areas, but a magnet does not have to be a
particular shape for poles to occur. This strength at the poles is a result of the way that
the electrons align in the same direction in magnetic material; at the ends of the material,
there are billions of 'free poles' that can exert a powerful attractive effect on other
magnetic materials. It is possible to create two magnets by cutting a magnet in half, but
it's a difficult process as hammering or heating a magnet can cause it to de-magnetise.

Steel is usually used to make permanent magnets, as it retains its magnetism much
better than other materials. Magnets are made by exposing steel to an electric current,
which aligns the magnetic fields of the electrons in the metal. And the opposite can
happen – electricity can be made by moving magnets near a wire. An understanding of
this relationship between electricity and magnetism has enabled the construction of
electric motors and turbines.

TALKING POINTS: LIGHT AND SHADOW

Talking Points

Think together to share everyone's ideas and decide what you will say to the class.

1 Light can be made from electricity.

2 Light can be different colours.

3 White light is made up of a mixture of light of different colours.

4 We can see shadows every day.

5 Shadows are the same shape as the thing they are next to.

6 Shadows are biggest in the middle of the day.

7 A shadow is made of black dust.

8 A shadow cannot change its shape.

9 Shadows get darker in the day and lighter in the evening.

10 You can get coloured shadows.

11 Shadows stick to our feet.

12 The sun gives us light every day.

13 The moon changes shape because of its own shadow.

THINKING TOGETHER

Think together to draw and label a stick, upright in the ground, on a sunny day. Show how the shadow changes and say why. Think of somewhere where the size and shape of a shadow will not change during the day and find a way to explain this.

Information: Light and shadow

Light is a form of **energy** that radiates from a **source**.
Sources of light range from the sun to chemically created
phosphorescence in insects and deep-sea fish, to electrical
discharges of lightning in the sky. Light sources can be
created, such as when electricity powers a bulb. Such
primary light sources can be distinguished from objects that
reflect or scatter light, such as the Moon. Reflectors are
secondary light sources.

Light is considered to travel as waves. White light is made up
of a mix of different wavelengths. Each wavelength appears to us as a different colour
when light splits into a spectrum. However, if we want to explain photosynthesis, or the
fading of paper in sunlight, we consider light as particles (or **photons**) – small 'packets'
of energy.

Light travels in straight lines. An opaque object blocks the light source and an area of
darkness or shadow is formed. The 'sharpness' of the shadow depends upon the
strength of the light source and the presence of ambient light. For example, on bright
sunny days shadows are usually sharp, whereas, on a cloudy day, sunlight is diffused by
and reflected from the clouds, leading to hazy-edged shadows. Shadow size is affected
by how close an object is to the light source. Shadow shape and direction are affected
by the angle of the light source to the object, as we see when looking at a sundial.

Changes to the Moon's shape – known as the phases of the Moon – depend on its
position in relation to the Sun and Earth. The same side of the Moon is always facing the
Earth; we never see its far side. As the Moon makes its way around the Earth, we see
the sunlit disc of the Moon's surface from different angles. The Moon 'changes shape'
because sometimes we can only see a part of the moon lit by the sun. A full Moon
happens once every 28 days. As the Moon swings around the earth, for about two
weeks we see a waning Moon, as we see less of the lit face and more of it is in shadow
every day. Then, after a night of no Moon at all, we cannot see it because no sunlight is
falling on the side of the moon that is always turned towards the earth – we see a little
more of the Moon every day for about a fortnight, a waxing Moon, until the next full
Moon.

The shadow of the Earth does fall on the Moon sometimes, during a lunar eclipse.
An eclipse of the Moon can only occur at full Moon and only if the Moon passes
through some portion of Earth's shadow. The Sun, Earth and Moon align only relatively
rarely.

TALKING POINTS: SOUND

Talking Points

Think together to decide whether these ideas are true, false, or you are unsure. Make sure you ask one another for reasons for ideas.

1   Sound is caused by something vibrating.

2   If you want to make a drum or guitar sound louder, you must use more force.

3   To make a note from a guitar string sound higher (that is, have a higher pitch) you have to re-tune by turning the peg to tighten the string.

4   If a drum skin is stretched less tightly, the drum sound will have a lower pitch.

5   If you were outside a space ship on a space walk, the sound of the rocket would be very loud.

6   You cannot hear in water, which is why fish don't speak.

7   Sound travels better through metal than through wood or air.

8   We hear sounds through our ears because air carries the vibration to the ear.

9   Sound travels very rapidly.

10   Sound and light move at the same speed.

11   Sound and light are both forms of energy.

12   Understanding sound is important in some people's jobs.

THINKING TOGETHER

Think together to draw and label a picture of inside the human ear to show how ears work. Add information that explains about protecting your hearing.

Information: Sound

Sound, like light, is a form of **energy**. Sound is generated by a vibrating source. Sound needs to travel in a **medium** – a solid, liquid or gas. This is unlike light, which can travel through a vacuum such as the empty space between the Earth and the Sun. The classic experiment to establish that sound can't travel in a vacuum is placing a clockwork alarm in a bell jar and gradually removing the air with a vacuum pump; when there is no more air, no sound can be heard, despite the fact that the striker can still be seen hitting the bells of the clock.

Sound travels in air at around 330 m per second, which is about a million times more slowly than light. In liquids and solids, sound travels a little faster. This is because the **molecules** of liquids and solids are more closely packed than in a gas and so can transfer energy more readily. That is, the **denser** the medium, the better the sound energy can travel. We hear sounds differently in water than in air. Sound energy from a vibrating source radiates in waves in all directions. Molecules of the medium (solid, liquid or gas) carry the waves, which gradually diminish the further away they are from the vibrating source. This happens because, as the molecules of the medium hit one another, some of the energy is 'lost' as heat.

Sound waves have two main characteristics – **frequency** and **amplitude**. Frequency refers to how many vibrations there are per second, measured in **hertz** (1 vibration in 1 second = 1 Hz). The frequency of the sound wave determines the **pitch** of the sound; high pitch corresponds to high frequency while low pitch corresponds to low frequency. The shorter the length of a string, the higher the pitch it will play when plucked; the shorter a vibrating column of air, the higher its pitch. Piccolos are smaller than bassoons, and play higher notes. With a string or a drum skin, the thinner or tighter it is, the higher the pitch. We can hear sounds with frequencies of about 30 Hz–20 kHz, although as you get older the ability to hear higher frequencies diminishes. By contrast, many animals can hear much higher frequencies and **bats** are truly exceptional. Their **echolocation** pulses can be anything between 20 and 200 kHz.

Amplitude determines the volume of a sound, which is measured in decibels (dB). With musical instruments, amplitude can increase if more force is used – for example, a string being plucked more aggressively, a pipe being blown harder, a drum being struck harder. A whisper has a volume of about 1 dB, while a vacuum cleaner has a volume of about 70 dB. Around 100 dB sound is potentially damaging over time, while single sounds above 110 dB are at the threshold of pain and may be potentially damaging even if experienced infrequently. A plane taking off has a volume of about 130 dB.

TALKING POINTS: OUR PLACE IN SPACE

Talking Points

Share everyone's ideas and decide on a group idea. Are the ideas here true, or false, or is your group unsure? Uncertainty is helpful for learning! Make sure everyone is asked to say what they think and why.

1   A light year is a measure of distance.

2   It takes eight minutes for light from the Sun to reach the Earth.

3   The heat of the Sun comes from burning rock.

4   The Sun goes round the Earth once a year.

5   The Earth looks blue from space because the sky is blue.

6   Space is very close to the Earth's surface – only about 60 miles up.

7   The Moon shines because it is alight.

8   There is a thin layer of air around the Moon.

9   The Moon changes shape because it is in the shadow of the Earth.

10   Jupiter is made up of clouds of ice and hydrogen gas.

11   The rings of Saturn are made of rainbows of light.

12   Venus is nearly the same size as Earth.

13   It is dark at night because the Moon is blocking out the Sun.

14   Some nights, you can see Jupiter, Venus or Mars quite easily.

15   The Moon has no gravity.

THINKING TOGETHER

Think together to draw and label a picture of the solar system, saying how the planets move and what each looks like. Add any other features of the solar system that you know about.

Information: Our place in space

(See also the sections of this book on forces, and light and shadow.)

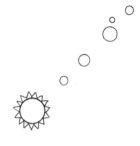

The Sun has a diameter of 1,392,000 km (as opposed to the Earth's 12,756 km and the Moon's tiny 3,476 km). The Sun is 333,000 times heavier than the Earth; as a ball of hot gas that continuously generates heat and light by **nuclear fusion**. During every minute, it converts 240 million tonnes of mass into energy; and the surface (called the **photosphere**) is a fairly constant 5,500 °C, while, at the core, it is around 14 million °C. It contains nearly all of the matter in the solar system and the **gravitational force of attraction** between the sun and other objects in the **solar system** essentially holds the system together. Light from the Sun, travelling at about 300,000 km/s, takes over eight minutes to get to Earth. A light year is a distance, not a time – the distance light can travel, in a vacuum such as space, in a year.

But amazing as the Sun is, the Earth is even more amazing. As far as we are aware, it is the only planet anywhere that has life. The combination of water, an oxygen and nitrogen-based atmosphere, and diverse weather patterns enables an almost inconceivable variety of plant and animal life to flourish. From space, Earth is the 'blue planet', a phenomenon that results from the fact that about 70 per cent of the earth's surface is covered in water. Earth is the only planet that we know of where water exists in liquid form on the surface, making it accessible to living things (but most of the Earth's water is frozen or salty so it is undrinkable). Other planets may be bigger and more mysterious – such as Jupiter, the gas giant, or Saturn with its rings of water ice extending hundreds of thousands of kilometres from the planet – but Earth seems to be utterly unique in the universe.

The Moon is connected to the Earth by **gravity**. Revolving counter-clockwise round the Earth in an **elliptical orbit** that takes just over 27 days, the distance of the Moon from the Earth varies between about 360,000 and 400,000 km. The gravitational forces between the Moon and the Earth create the **tides**, which are partly explained by the fact that the moon causes a 'bulge' of water through its gravitational attraction.

TALKING POINTS: SOLIDS, LIQUIDS AND GASES

Talking Points

We can think of everything on earth as made up of tiny, invisible particles. Think together to draw and label (annotate) some cartoon particle diagrams.

1 Draw cartoon particles of these materials:

- hydrogen
- water
- sugar
- an element (gold or silver particles for example)
- a mixture (particles of salt and water for example)
- a compound (some water molecules).

2 Draw particles of water to show how they are arranged in ice (solid), water (liquid) and steam (gas). Annotate the drawings to explain how:

- solids keep the same volume and shape
- liquids keep the same volume but can change shape
- gases can change volume and change shape.

3 Draw cartoons of particles to show what happens in:

- evaporation
- condensation
- melting
- freezing
- boiling.

4 Draw cartoons to show what happens when you try to compress a solid (a rock), then a liquid (water in a syringe), and finally a gas (air).

5 Draw these materials as cartoon particles, each with a speech bubble to say whether they are solid, liquid or gas, and why.

- plastic
- syrup
- sawdust
- shaving foam
- plasticine
- wood
- wire
- balloon
- tomato sauce
- custard
- glass
- wire
- flour.

6 Draw a picture of water particles starting as ice then changing to water then steam . . . and back again . . . showing what happens when heat energy is added . . . and then removed.

TALKING POINTS: FINDING OUT ABOUT A RANGE OF MATERIALS

- glass
- jelly and custard
- metals
- nitrogen, oxygen and carbon dioxide
- plastics
- rocks and soils
- water
- wood, cardboard, cork and paper
- wool and cotton

Talking Points

With your group, think together to:

1   Choose a material from the list and find out as much as you can about it.

2   Prepare a presentation in which each group member presents in turn.

> Your presentation should:
>
> - describe the material;
> - say how it is manufactured or purified;
> - describe its properties,
> - explain its uses related to its properties; and
> - if possible, provide actual everyday examples.

You will be asked to **evaluate your group performance** by providing examples of effective group work such as:

- information sharing;
- supporting one another's thinking;
- negotiating ideas;
- listening;
- providing positive feedback;
- asking useful questions; and
- staying on task.

Presentation session

3   Take notes, evaluate and summarise.

THINKING TOGETHER

During the presentation, you will observe the presentation of another group, taking notes. After the presentations, think together to write about:

- your understanding of a material based on what you have seen and heard;
- a positive evaluation of the presentation focussing on what you've learned from classmates; and
- the use of talk for learning in science.

4   Use your presentation to:

- contribute to a classroom **display**;
- compile a **quiz**;
- devise a set of ten **Talking Points**;
- **draw annotated cartoon particles** to show key properties of the material.

5   Evaluate your group talk and group work. What adjustments are needed to the Ground Rules for Talk; what can you suggest to help others work well together; what are the advantages of talk groups for science or for other classroom work; what are the disadvantages; how do you like to learn; what other topics can you research for presentation to the rest of your class or the school?

TALKING POINTS: MATERIALS AND THE SENSES

Talking Points

Our five senses help us to say which material is which. Think together to decide on some descriptive words that will say exactly how we can tell one material from another.

	jam	glass	air	water	chocolate
touch					
smell					
taste					
hearing					
sight					

THINKING TOGETHER

Think together about each of our senses separately. What do we actually notice? Think of some describing words to explain your ideas.

	ice	fire	wool	jelly	fur
touch					

	ice cream	fireworks	soup	jelly	shoes
smell					

	ice cream	lemon	water	strawberry	medicine
taste					

	birds	traffic	voices	music	water
hearing					

	sky	sea	mirror	dust	metal
sight					

TALKING POINTS: WATER

Talking Points

What are your ideas about water and the water supply? Share your ideas about the Talking Points so that you can provide the class with a joint, reasoned opinion.

1 Water is free.

2 There is plenty of water for everyone.

3 Water is good for you.

4 Drinking water and water to wash in should be clean.

5 Water is used once then goes back to the sea.

6 Water from rain is clean water.

7 Bottled water is a good idea.

8 Our drinking water comes from the nearest lake or reservoir.

9 We don't use much water at home and in school.

10 The sea is clean; we just need to take the salt out of sea water to drink it.

11 Water supply in the UK is not a problem; other countries have huge problems with water supply.

THINKING TOGETHER

Find out as much as you can about where your drinking water comes from, and what happens to waste water. Annotate the water cycle diagram to show how water moves around the world. Think about all the things that happen during your day that use water. We should be careful not to waste water; add your ideas why, and show how you can try to use less water.

Water cycle

Talking Points for history

Talking Points can allow children to express their points of view and to share factual information. Some children love history and have an extensive knowledge of various times, places and people. It is terrific to enable them to act as class expert and, at the same time, extend their own thinking.

In this section, there are three history topics. Each provides a different structure for examining facts, thinking about historical issues, and animating the lives of people who lived in previous times. The group activities are inclusive and rely on children collaborating to create joint outcomes.

You can adapt these structures to generate talk-focused activities for any topic your class is studying.

THE GEORGIANS

Groups are asked to create a three-minute play or storyboard to share with the whole class. To do so, they must think about their own lives in comparison to the lives lived by some Georgians.

THE VIKINGS

Groups are asked to consider some ideas about Viking life, to decide which they think are 'true' and which they believe to be false. They must draw on their understanding of Viking life and times to come to a joint agreement that they can defend with reasons.

THE INCAS

Groups are asked to research information about one aspect of Inca life. They then put this understanding to use by generating a drawing, play or other creative work that will help them to share what they have discovered with the rest of the class. They also generate some Talking Points that will stimulate discussion about their topic.

TALKING POINTS: THE GEORGIANS

Imagine that you are part of a family living in Georgian times. Use exploratory talk to discuss these ideas. Find out everyone's opinions and reasons. What do you think these families might not have considered as they faced the future?

Create a three-minute play or storyboard that you can share with the whole class.

The farmer's family Steam engines that can plant seeds and help with the harvest are a really good idea. We can do without so many farm workers if we can use machines instead. Life will be a lot easier for us without all that backbreaking planting, hoeing and harvesting. Perhaps we should stop paying the workers their wages. They can go and find work in town. We will be much happier with machines instead.

The coal merchant's family Canals are a great advantage and will help everyone to have an easier life. We can load coal on to canal barges and take it to where it is needed, in the mills. We can live on the barge. We will not be dependent on anyone else. Canals are so much more efficient than carriages for transport. There is nothing to beat them. Living on a canal boat is going to be easy and comfortable.

The farm worker's family It is good that there are new big factories where we can all go to work and earn our living. We are going to move to a city where there are proper houses instead of damp, tumbledown cottages to live in. We will probably become rich and have many luxuries, and wear new clothes. We will eat meat instead of turnips and rye bread. The factory work is going to be easier than working on the land. This is progress.

The weaver's family We wonder if the new weaving machines will make much difference. People will always need the cloth we make for clothes. Maybe we can ignore the new weaving looms and carry on working on our hand loom at home, as we have always done. Anyway, if they build a weaving factory near here, we will go and work there – we have the skills.

The trader's family Of course we have an elegant house in Bath, and a stately home in extensive park lands. We have none of these crowded workers' houses on our land. We will not let the railway come through our park land. We have a Member of Parliament we choose ourselves, to help rule the country; there is no need for anyone to vote for him. Things have to stay like they are because we know best how to keep the country rich and trading successfully with other nations. The workers do not know how to make laws and organise everybody to make money – they should not be allowed to vote.

Information: The Georgians

The Georgian Kings ruled Britain for 123 years, from 1714 until 1837. This included the reign of King George I, King George II, King George IV and William IV.

Before the 1730s, most people worked on the land, or worked at home.

The first steam engines that could work machines were made in the early 1700s. Large factories were built and people moved to live near them and work with the machines. Machines were used for mining coal, making cloth and making other goods to be sold. Also in the early 1700s, machines to plant and harvest crops were invented.

People could grow more food. Cities began to expand. People moved away from the land to live in crowded housing with no proper water supply or drains. Small houses were home to large families, with an outside water pump for the whole neighbourhood, and outside earth toilets.

By the early 1800s, canals had been built. This meant that goods could be moved around more readily. Previously, the fastest method of travel was by horse-drawn carriage. Roads that were very muddy and full of holes were repaired by the late 1700s. The stagecoach taking passengers from London to Edinburgh took two weeks in 1745; by 1796, the same journey only took two and a half days. Ships were built with steam-powered engines, carrying goods and passengers between the coastal cities. Railways became the main transport in the 1800s. Rail travel began when steam engines mounted on wheels were used to pull a train of carriages and goods wagons. By the mid-1840s, hundreds of miles of railway lines had been laid down.

Most children did not go to school. Better-off families paid for tutors who lived with them and taught their sons until they were old enough to go to boarding schools. Girls were taught by a governess who would instruct them how to sew, paint and play the piano; they were not considered to need an education that would lead to them qualifying for University or being able to get a job. Girls were expected to marry someone who would support them financially. Men had to earn enough to support their wives and families. Children of poorer families started work from the age of 6. Their jobs in factories were tasks such as crawling under the working machines to clean them; farm work involved working in the fields at all times of the year; working in the mines meant being underground all the hours of daylight, dragging trucks along.

In 1833, it became illegal to make children under 12 work in cloth factories, and in 1842 the employment of women and children in underground mines was stopped.

TALKING POINTS: THE VIKINGS

Talking Points

What do you think of the Viking way of life? Share your ideas and understanding of the Vikings by discussing these points.

1   The Vikings were aggressive, violent warriors.

2   Vikings travelled because they wanted to steal silver and gold.

3   'Vikings' were not a tribe, but lawless pirates from several countries.

4   The Vikings who landed in Britain tried to destroy Christianity.

5   The Christian monks in Britain were corrupt and wealthy and deserved to be attacked.

6   Viking men and women were thought of as equals.

7   Vikings travelled to get away from the cold climate and poor farmland of their own country.

8   Children were sacrificed if their fathers thought it would persuade the gods to help them win a battle – this was cruel.

9   Clothes were made of natural materials.

10   The number of Viking rings, bracelets and brooches found shows that they were vain.

11   Vikings could write and read.

12   The way Vikings lived was dependent on the weather.

13   Children did not go to school so were not taught anything.

14   Viking men did not wash, and never did the washing up.

15   Viking women were just housewives.

THINKING TOGETHER

Draw a Viking home together. Think about who would live there, what they would be doing, and what possessions everyone would have. Think of three reasons you would like to live there, and three reasons you would prefer to stay in the present.

Information: The Vikings

Viking is a Norse term for men who were travellers and pirates. The Vikings were warriors, and they were also craftsmen, sailors and farmers. They travelled from Denmark, Norway and Sweden to other countries in the northern hemisphere. Originally, they believed in many gods, such as Odin, the god of poetry, death and battle; when a Viking died in battle, a warrior maiden called a Valkyrie took him to a kind of heaven called Valhalla. Frey was the god of harvest and his sister Freya the goddess of love. Vikings believed that sacrifice could alter events. Anything of value could be offered as a sacrifice – even children. By AD 1100, the Vikings converted to Christianity.

Vikings took goods such as furs, walrus ivory, falcons and iron to trade with other countries. They travelled by sea and would either trade with local people or raid their villages. For three centuries, the Vikings raided towns and monasteries in Europe. They took over villages and lands, settling in Shetland and the north of Scotland, and then other parts of Britain, Ireland, Greenland and other countries.

Viking men were farmers, hunters and boat builders. They valued battle skills such as the ability to shoot arrows, hunt with hounds or fight with a sword; they enjoyed wrestling as a test of strength. Vikings were expected to always have ready a sword or axe, a spear, a bow and arrows, and an iron helmet, and maybe even a mail shirt. Men were responsible for providing the family with food and shelter.

Viking women were traders and organisers, responsible for farms and villages while men were away on sea voyages. Women travelled to new colonies in Greenland, Iceland and Vinland (Canada). They made woollen cloth and organised the dairy work and harvesting, and used weights and measures to conduct trade in precious metals and jewels. They reared children and kept the homes and farms running. Some women were scholars, involved in promoting Christianity. Women were responsible for ensuring food was stored for the long cold winter.

Poorer Viking men and women were slaves; the better off were merchants and weavers, and there were also rich aristocratic families.

Viking boats were used for fishing, war and travel. Longboats were made of oak bound together with leather thongs. The longboats were very fast in the water, with the oars aided by large square sails. Viking raiders were aggressive and ruthless, destroying homes and farms, stealing women and children, and killing anyone opposed to them. Monasteries were targeted because the monks had golden treasure, and were often poorly defended. Northern and eastern England were conquered by a band of Vikings with a raven on their flag, known as the Host. In AD 878, King Alfred successfully attacked the Host and forced the Vikings to surrender. But raiding bands of Host continued to attack northern France, Belgium and Germany. Knut of Denmark eventually conquered England and became king.

TALKING POINTS: THE INCAS

THINKING TOGETHER

For these research topics, think together to draw a storyboard, poster or annotated cartoon, or produce a presentation or web pages, with some Talking Points.

Money The Incas did not use money. They worked together, accepted the rule of a leader, and shared food and goods without paying for anything or getting any wages. Think together to decide how you would explain the idea of money to an Inca person the same age as yourselves. Think how you could explain the uses, advantages and disadvantages of money. Decide how you would describe the different currencies of the world. Make up three Talking Points that will help others to think about the important points of your presentation.

Machu Picchu Machu Picchu was an Inca city high in the Andes that became deserted for hundreds of years after the Spaniards arrived. It was re-discovered in 1911. At its heart is the Intihuatana stone. At the spring and autumn equinoxes (21 March and 21 September), the sun stands almost directly above the stone at midday. Think together to draw and annotate a description of the stone, its surroundings, and how it was used by the Inca people in their ceremonies. Make up three Talking Points that will help others to think about the important points of your presentation.

The Inca system of government The Inca system worked on the idea of *reciprocity*. Reciprocity means sharing with others, or depending on others and letting others depend on you. So, things such as woollen cloth or metal ploughs that were made in one area were taken to other areas in exchange for other things, food, or services such as road building. Everyone shared what they had, contributing what they made or grew, and getting from others things that they needed but could not make. Design a diagram drawn by an Inca showing how goods, services and food were moved between villages, and how people depended on one another. Make up three Talking Points that will help others to think about the important points of your presentation.

Homes and family life The Incas had simple homes and few possessions. Think together to decide how you would explain a modern home to an Inca person the same age as yourselves. Draw an Inca home and think about what it would be like to live in it, deciding what you would like about it and what might be difficult. Think about children's lives and draw cartoons to show how Inca children contributed to their society. Make up three Talking Points that will help others to think about the important points of your presentation.

Information: The Incas

By AD 1200, the Incas had established a thriving civilisation in South America, around the town of Cuzco in Peru. There were about 6 million Incas living in a wide area from the Andes Mountains to the Pacific Ocean coast. The Incas increased the amount of flat land available for crops in the mountains by constructing terraces. They built canals to irrigate their crops and grew maize, grain and potatoes.

The first Inca leader, Manco Capac, claimed that the sun was his father; after him, all Inca leaders were known as 'Sons of the Sun'. Ordinary people were expected to fear and respect the leadership and authority of the ruling family, who lived in luxurious palaces surrounded by guards. The people paid labour taxes. They had to work for up to five years in the mines or in the army, or join gangs to build public houses or roads. Ordinary people worked hard but could expect to be properly clothed, have enough food and live in a straightforward house.

Girls were taught weaving and sewing, and they looked after the family babies and helped in the house. They collected firewood and made the food. They helped to gather the fine wool from alpacas and vicunas to make a woven cloth for clothing and blankets. Boys learned how to grow food and to use tools for building and animal work, and some of them learned to work with gold and other precious metals such as silver, copper and tin. Children helped to increase the amount of food by scaring birds and animals away from the crops, and helping to water the corn.

Inca houses in the mountains were made of stone, carefully chiselled to fit together, and roofed with wood and straw. Houses nearer the ocean were made of a mix of mud and straw shaped into bricks that were hardened by baking in the sun. There was little furniture and people slept on the floor, wrapped in their blankets. Families lived in a single room, spending most of their time outdoors.

The rich leaders lived a very different life than the poorer workers. As a society, Incas were successful in developing skills in agriculture, metalwork, ceramics, building and fabric work, as well as gaining a living from some very harsh environments such as the high Andes and the deserts near the coast.

The Spanish began to explore the Pacific coast in the 1520s. Within a few years, they had captured and killed the Inca leaders and enslaved the Inca people, carried off the Inca gold and colonised the lands. Peru today has a population of people of Spanish and Inca descent. A famous story tells of the Inca King Atahualpa inviting a group of Spaniards to meet with him. He was 36 years old. He was captured and taken prisoner. To try to escape death, he offered to fill an entire room to more than his own height with gold objects; his captors took the gold, but kept him imprisoned. Eventually, he was executed and the Spaniards took over the country, introducing the ideas of money, slavery and Roman Catholic Christianity. They also brought European diseases. The Inca empire was destroyed by the effects of war and disease.

Lots to talk about

Talking Points in this section encourage discussion about the following informal themes:

- **Ourselves and others**
- **The world around us**
- **Music**
- **Works of art.**

Creating 'Lots to talk about' Talking Points for your class

There are always things that a class could helpfully discuss; teachers are well aware of what their class needs. Talking Points help the class to stay focused on what is important. Discussion can bring out a range of points of view, reasoned opinions, factual information, and misconceptions. Talk with others can foster children's curiosity and become the starting point for a personal quest for understanding.

Once you have decided on a subject or thought of a picture, piece of music, or a theme, collect ideas by asking individual children what they would like to discuss. Search web pages and books for facts or ideas that you think will stimulate talk. Rephrase ideas in your own words for clarity and brevity.

For example, when thinking about the 'time' Talking Points, I came across this sentence on Wikipedia:

> The past is the set of events that can send light signals to the observer; the future is the set of events to which the observer can send light signals.

This reminded me of the famous first sentence of L.P. Hartley's novel, *The Go Between*:

> The past is a foreign country; they do things differently there.

And these are the ensuing Talking Points:

1 The past is events we remember; the future is events we cannot yet see.
2 People did things differently in the past.

Children may agree or disagree with these statements; either is good!

TALKING POINTS: WAYS OF LEARNING

Talking Points

How do we learn? Think together to share your ideas.

1   When it comes to skills, practice makes perfect.

2   Criticism from others helps, but encouragement helps even more.

3   Learning needs to have some reward like a sticker or time off.

4   Rewards are unfair because, if you can't do something, it is not your fault.

5   You can't understand some things until you are old enough.

6   If you don't understand something, you are obviously not very clever.

7   When starting something new, it's useful to think about what you already know.

8   You have to be able to explain something to show that you understand it.

9   You can learn from just about anyone.

10   You can learn facts, but you have to think of your own ideas.

11   Some people have a better memory than others; you can't do anything about it.

12   To learn about something, you have to be interested.

13   It's hard to learn when everyone is talking.

14   Talking to classmates helps learning.

15   School learning is different from learning at home.

16   How well you learn depends a lot on how you feel.

17   Listening is a very difficult skill.

18   Sometimes it is really impossible to concentrate.

THINKING TOGETHER

Talk with your group and draw a diagram that shows how people working together can help each other. Add information to show how people might also stop each other doing their best.

54

TALKING POINTS: LISTENING

Talking Points

Discuss these ideas about listening with your group. Think about your ideas and the points of view your friends share with you. Can you come to an agreement?

1 Listening is never easy.

2 Sometimes it is very important to listen.

3 To listen properly, you have to sit still.

4 It is hard to listen in a noisy room, especially if other people are talking or playing computer games.

5 Some people seem to like listening; others don't.

6 You can listen without thinking.

7 Sometimes, listening is important for safety reasons.

8 Listening to music is different from listening to talk.

9 You can only listen properly for two minutes. After that, your mind wanders.

10 Your mind wanders because listening is boring.

11 Boring means 'hard to understand' or 'uninteresting'.

12 If you think while you listen, you remember things better.

13 Some people are easier to listen to than others.

14 To concentrate means to empty your mind of other things, and think about the present.

15 Some people never listen.

16 By listening, you can learn facts or find out about other people's opinions.

17 Ideas become clearer when people talk and listen to each other.

18 Listening helps creativity.

19 You can learn how to listen, just like you can learn to read or write.

THINKING TOGETHER

Draw and label a cartoon of someone listening, and someone who never listens.

TALKING POINTS: FRIENDS

Talking Points

Share your ideas. Listen carefully and build on what others say.

1   You only really need one good friend.

2   Friends are people you never fall out with.

3   Friends can sometimes be really difficult.

4   Friends can help you.

5   It is hard to make new friends.

6   Once you fall out with a friend, you never trust them again.

7   If you have two friends, they will be friends with each other.

8   It is quite difficult to have family and friends together.

9   Friends can sometimes do things that are very hard to understand.

10 It's difficult to do school work with friends because you want to talk instead.

11 Some friends seem to make you do things you would not do without them.

12 There are some people you would like to be friends with, but it seems impossible.

13 Some people are just unfriendly.

14 Quiet people are unfriendly.

15 Unpopular people don't need friends.

16 Bullies don't have friends – that is why they need to be bullies.

17 Friends never let you down.

18 A friend would always try to do their best for you.

THINKING TOGETHER

Draw a cartoon picture of 'the ideal friend'. Label your picture with ideas about what a friend does, thinks, knows, and says; and how they make you think and feel.

TALKING POINTS: HANDS

Talking Points

**Discuss these ideas. Do you agree with them?
What do you know about hands? Share your
thinking.**

1 People can talk with their hands.

2 Hands can become skilful through practice; for example, learning to play a
musical instrument.

3 Anything you want to do well with your hands needs time and practice.

4 We can each say what we are good at with our hands.

5 Hands are the same size as each other.

6 Hands and feet are the same size.

7 Hands can show such emotions as aggression, friendliness, uncertainty, or
fear.

8 You can clap your hands in different ways to show different things.

9 Using a keyboard to type is easier than using a pen or pencil to write.

10 You can use hands to mime many different activities or jobs.

11 You can use hands to show a range of different animals.

12 You can have an ambition about what you might
want to get better at doing with your hands.

13 The hands each have twenty bones.

14 Each finger has a name.

15 Nails grow all the time, even when you are asleep.

16 Joints in the fingers are called hinge joints and are
held together by ligaments.

17 Being left-handed is a real problem.

18 It's the way our thumbs work that makes hands so
useful for doing a wide variety of jobs.

19 Shaking hands, saluting and waving are helpful hand
gestures.

**THINKING
TOGETHER**

Draw round your
hands. Cut out
the shapes and
on them draw or
write all the
things you can
do with your
hands. Share
ideas with your
group. Make a
display.

TALKING POINTS: PLACES WE LIKE

INSTRUCTIONS

Read and listen: Choose who will read these instructions and the Thinking Together idea aloud.

1   Thinking Time

Before you start reading the **Thinking Together Activity**, choose who will talk first after the **thinking time**. Everyone will have a chance to talk, so the order doesn't really matter, but must be decided in advance so that worrying about it doesn't stop the discussion. How will you do this? By discussion; by throwing a dice or drawing straws; by alphabet order of names; any way that is quick and definite.

2   Talk Time

During **talk time**, everyone else must listen and think of questions to help the speaker. Pass on the turn to talk after about a minute.

3   Question Time

After everyone has had a chance to talk, take time to ask each other questions, discuss your ideas, and come to group decisions about the Talking Points.

THINKING TOGETHER ACTIVITY

Talk about a place you like. Give some reasons why you like it, and some reasons why you think other people in your group might like it too.

Listen to others as they describe their special place.

Question Time: Places we like

Ask each other questions to find out more about the places you have heard about. Try to find out more about the place, and about why your group mates like it. Try to decide if you might like it too.

Talking Points

Does your group agree or disagree with these ideas? Can you give reasons for your decision?

1 We have listened attentively to each other talking about interesting places.

2 We can say what reasons other people have for liking their special place.

3 We have heard of somewhere where it would be good to go.

4 We can give an example of a good reason for liking a place.

5 We can come to a decision about what is similar about all the places we have described.

6 We can think of some important differences between the places.

7 We can suggest other people who might like to visit the places, and give reasons.

8 Our discussion helped us to see why different people like different things.

9 We found it difficult to describe things to each other.

10 We found it difficult to listen.

11 We could not think of any reasons, or any helpful questions.

12 We would have liked the chance to talk and listen for longer.

THINKING TOGETHER

Draw a Venn diagram, list or picture that shows similarities and differences between the places each of you described.

TALKING POINTS: MONEY

Talking Points

Talk together to share your ideas. Listen carefully and think about the reasons others give. Can you work towards a group agreement to share with the whole class?

1 Money causes a lot of problems for people.

2 Money does not make people happy.

3 Everyone should have enough money, but not too much.

4 It is important to have rich people because they support all sorts of charities to help others.

5 Poor people are lazy.

6 All children the same age should have the same pocket money.

7 We can think of things to do with the money if we won the lottery.

8 There is never a good reason to steal money.

9 Some people, such as footballers, get paid too much.

10 If you have a problem, money usually helps.

11 A sensible ambition is to get rich.

THINKING TOGETHER

Your school wins £100 on the lottery! Think together to decide how it might best be used by your class or school. Can you identify any problems or disadvantages of being awarded this money?

TALKING POINTS: TIME

Talking Points

What does your group think of these ideas?
Share everything you know.

1 Some people have more time to do things than others.

2 Time goes quickly when you are having fun.

3 Time goes more slowly at night.

4 There is never enough time to everything you want to do.

5 Sometimes, time goes by incredibly slowly.

6 We are all ruled by the time on the clock.

7 Telling the time is a useful skill to learn.

8 Time is made by the Earth going round.

9 A minute is a long time if you are trying to do something difficult.

10 We can think of some common sayings to do with time.

11 Time is an imaginary idea made up to help us put things in order.

12 Time flows like sand moves in a sand timer.

13 Time flies.

14 The earth is split into a number of different time zones.

15 Australia celebrates the new year eleven hours before the UK.

16 The past is events we remember; the future is events we cannot yet see.

17 People did things differently in the past.

18 The past cannot be changed, but the future can.

19 Now is the only important time, and we should make the most of it.

20 We all have the same amount of time in a day, and have to decide how to use it.

21 It is not possible to 'waste time' – every experience is important.

THINKING TOGETHER

Draw a time line for a day and agree on how you would like to spend the time.

TALKING POINTS: PLAY

Talking Points

Think about all sorts of play and games. When do you like playing, and what sort of things or people help you to enjoy play? How would you explain play to a Martian? Decide on your group's response to the Talking Points.

1   Play is important for learning.

2   Everyone can play; it just means doing things in a fun way.

3   You need expensive toys to help you play.

4   Playing outside is more fun than playing inside.

5   Playing outside is something children used to do in the past.

6   There are some games that children know but adults don't.

7   We can say what our favourite games and toys are.

8   Computer games were invented to keep children quiet.

9   It is more fun to play on a computer than any other sort of game.

10   You need lots of friends to play.

11   Sometimes it is hard to think of interesting things to do.

12   Play is a waste of time.

13   We could suggest some helpful things to play with in the classroom.

14   Some people are really good at making up games.

15   Some people don't seem to know how to play and always ruin games.

16   Games need rules.

17   A time machine would be a good idea.

18   Play is relaxing.

19   Only little children play.

20   Everyone likes break time.

THINKING TOGETHER

Draw and label the ideal playground. Be ready to justify your ideas.

62

TALKING POINTS: PETS

Talking Points

Talk together to share your ideas about pets your family has had and what makes a good pet.

1   Pets are expensive.

2   Pets do not live long.

3   Pets are a lot of work.

4   Pets create lots of arguments in families.

5   Some pets are better than others.

6   Some animals are friendly and others are hard to understand.

7   Some people have pets just to show off.

8   Some people are cruel to pets and should be banned from owning animals.

9   Wild animals should not be kept as pets.

10 Dogs are only interested in food.

11 Most dogs need too much attention.

12 Dogs are pack animals and never really fit in as pets.

13 Cats are only interested in sleeping.

14 Cats should be banned because they catch so many birds.

15 Cats have been kept as pets for all of history.

16 Reptiles do nothing and should not be kept as pets.

17 If you have a pet and it dies, you can just get another.

18 Young children do not know how to care for gerbils or hamsters.

19 Any kind of cage is cruel and unnecessary.

20 Pets help people in lots of ways.

THINKING TOGETHER

Draw a group picture of pets that you like and label it to say why you like them.

63

TALKING POINTS: HEDGEHOGS

Talking Points

What do you think about hedgehogs? Talk about the ideas below to come to a group agreement that you can share with the class.

1 We have/have not seen a live hedgehog . . . or a wild hedgehog . . .

2 Hedgehogs are dirty and always have fleas.

3 Hedgehogs are not really important animals.

4 There were no hedgehogs on the island of South Uist in Scotland until people took them there. Now, they cause real damage by eating the eggs of rare birds that nest on the ground. The hedgehogs should be trapped and killed to protect the birds.

5 People should not put out food for hedgehogs because it encourages rats.

6 Hedgehogs are dangerous to road users at night. Drivers swerve to avoid them and can crash. So hedgehogs should be kept out of towns if possible.

7 Gardeners should not use pesticide, but should leave the slugs for the hedgehogs.

8 A hedgehog would make a good pet.

9 People who kick hedgehogs are impossible to understand.

10 Hedgehogs should be protected by law.

Further information

www.sttiggywinkles.org.uk/index.html

THINKING TOGETHER

Talk together to draw a garden that offers a good home for hedgehogs. Annotate your drawing with labels to show the important features.

Information: Hedgehogs

Hedgehogs are small mammals with distinctive spiny skin. They are found all over the UK, in woodland, farmland and in gardens. Hedgehogs live on a diet of creatures such as worms, snails, slugs and beetles. They like cat food and dog food, too. Their eyesight is rather weak, but they have a good sense of smell, which helps them find prey; they have sharp  teeth and strong jaws to crunch through the hard outer case of beetles or to crack snail shells. Hedgehogs tend not to bite people. They are afraid of people. If picked up or touched they will frown so much that their spiny skin covers their face; if even more worried, they will roll into a prickly ball. They can stay like this for hours.

Badgers, with their strong claws, can 'open' a hedgehog if they try hard enough. But the main problem for hedgehogs is that rolling into a ball is no defence against road traffic. Many hedgehogs are killed on the roads. The only reason we do not see the sad little remains of them more often is because they are fairly rare creatures now. As well as traffic, there are many reasons why hedgehogs find life difficult. The things they eat are garden pests, eating vegetables and flowers. Gardeners get rid of slugs, beetles, caterpillars, and so on by using pesticides to kill them. This has two effects: there is less food for hedgehogs to eat, and the things that they do eat may be poisonous. In addition, they need somewhere quiet and undisturbed to hibernate in winter and as a nest for when their babies arrive.

Tidy gardens, ploughed fields and managed woodland leave few places for a hedgehog to make a leaf-lined nest and huddle inside it for the coldest part of the year. Our machines damage hedgehogs too – lawnmowers and strimmers can be lethal to them. And, although most people like hedgehogs, some people treat them with cruelty; for example, some young people have been filmed kicking a hedgehog like a ball.

Hedgehogs wander around a large area at night, looking for food. They can swim, and climb walls and trees. They are nocturnal because they are safer in darkness, and the things they eat are often on the move at night.

Hedgehogs breed in early summer, and have litters of four to six young in June or July. Baby hedgehogs – hoglets – are pink and blind, and take time to grow their spines. The mother hedgehog has to protect and feed them. After a month or so, they are old enough to go out of the nest to find things to eat. They are very vulnerable and a female may only raise two or three hoglets in a year. Some hedgehogs have babies late in the year. Babies too small to hibernate properly are called autumn orphans. There are organisations, such as St Tiggywinkles, that rescue them and keep them safe over winter, ready to be let out into the wild in spring.

Hedgehogs may not be glamorous like tigers or exciting like wolves, but they live wild in Great Britain, and are unique and interesting mammals. They have been around for twenty million years, and are good at helping to remove pests from crops. They have their own unique part to play in the health of our environment.

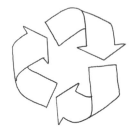

TALKING POINTS: RECYCLING

Talking Points

Does your group think recycling is important? What do you all do about recycling? Share your ideas.

1 Recycling paper is very important so that we do not have to cut down so many trees.

2 It is quite easy to get clean paper back from recycled paper.

3 Recycling is a nuisance and it is easier just to throw things away.

4 There is no such place as 'away'.

5 Recycling helps to keep places clean and tidy.

6 It is difficult to recycle cans when you are out; it is easier to put things in a bin.

7 People who throw litter out of cars should be punished.

8 Things made from recycled materials are dirty.

9 We can give examples of some recycled things that we can buy or that we use.

10 Recycling is something that only old people do.

11 We can draw the recycling logo.

12 'Reduce, re-use, recycle'. We can say what this means and why it matters.

13 Recycling is boring. Everyone does it so we do not need to think about it.

14 Most big companies waste so much paper that there is no point in us recycling ours.

15 For drinks, it might be better to have returnable bottles instead of ones you throw away.

16 Composting is a kind of recycling.

17 No one wants to wear recycled clothes.

18 We can give examples of things that we recycle at home or school.

THINKING TOGETHER

Draw a cartoon picture of trees being made into paper, which is used, recycled and used again.

66

TALKING POINTS: MUSIC

Talking Points

Do you think of yourself as 'musical?' Why is that? What are your ideas about different sorts of music? Share opinions and give reasons. Make sure that everyone is invited to say what they think.

1   Only people whose families play instruments learn to play instruments themselves.

2   Music can cheer you up.

3   Most music is really boring.

4   It's more fun playing music than listening to it.

5   Adults listen to music that children don't like.

6   It's easier to remember things if you make up a song about it.

7   Joining in with a chorus is embarrassing.

8   We can think of five different kinds of music.

9   Learning to play an instrument takes years and years, and is expensive.

10   Music is nothing to do with school.

11   In films, the music really matters.

12   Loud music is better than quiet music.

13   Girls like music more than boys do.

14   Everyone can sing.

15   Birds sing, so they must think in music.

THINKING TOGETHER

Draw a map of your school; use pictures to show where you might hear or play music. Use your map to make suggestions of where you think changes might be made. Use percussion instruments to make a sound picture to go with a poem, story or piece of art you are studying. Make sure everyone contributes and likes the part they are going to play. Perform your sound picture for your class.

TALKING POINTS: *WEEPING WOMAN* BY PABLO PICASSO

(To see this artwork, search Google Images for *Weeping Woman*.)

Talking Points

Look carefully at the picture. Think about what you observe, and share your ideas.

1 The lady is biting a handkerchief.

2 She has just heard some terrible news.

3 The news is probably to do with a person in her family.

4 She has no friend to help her.

5 Her face tells her story.

6 She is dressed to go out.

7 She bites her nails, showing that she is often worried.

8 People who cry are just feeling sorry for themselves.

9 She is a rich lady with an expensive haircut and designer clothes.

10 She can't be very upset or she wouldn't be wearing a red hat.

11 It's hard to feel sorry for someone you don't actually know.

12 You could cut up a print of this picture and stick it together to make an ordinary face.

13 The bright colours are very cheerful.

14 We can say what we like and dislike about this picture.

THINKING TOGETHER

Think together to make up a sympathetic story to explain why the lady is crying. Draw a storyboard.

TALKING POINTS: *THE BEDROOM AT ARLES* BY VINCENT VAN GOGH

(To see this artwork, search Google Images for *The Bedroom at Arles*.)

Talking Points

On 17 October 1888, Vincent Van Gogh wrote to his brother, Theo: 'I am adding a line to tell you that this afternoon I finished the canvas representing the bedroom.' He added that he thought his picture showed 'absolute restfulness'. Does your group agree with this, and with the Talking Points? For what reasons?

1   The walls are pale violet, the floor tiles red, and the chairs are yellow wood.

2   The scarlet bed cover looks warm.

3   The shutters are closed – they are green and let in some light.

4   There is no white in the picture.

5   There are no shadows but the room still looks real.

6   Vincent had very few possessions.

7   All his coats were blue.

8   Vincent enjoyed painting this picture.

9   He also painted the portraits he shows hanging on the walls.

10   The room does not look comfortable.

11   A room is not an interesting subject to paint.

THINKING TOGETHER

With your group, find out about Van Gogh's life at Arles. There are five versions of this picture. Find out when they were painted and look for similarities and differences.

TALKING POINTS: *THE SINGING BUTLER* BY JACK VETTRIANO

(To see this artwork, search Google Images for *The Singing Butler*.)

Talking Points

Do you and your group agree or disagree with these ideas?
For what reasons?

1   The couple dancing are very rich.
2   They are unhappy.
3   The man wants to dance and has made the lady join him.
4   Lots of things in the picture show that it is windy.
5   No one dances on a windy beach so this picture is an imaginary scene.
6   It is late evening in July, and the dance is a waltz.
7   The picture has lots of straight lines and lots of curved lines.
8   The maid is really fed up and cold and thinks her shoes are going to be ruined.
9   The butler is enjoying getting out of the house.
10   He has a good singing voice.
11   There is going to be a storm.
12   The tide is coming in.
13   There are only four people on the beach; or, behind the artist is a whole crowd of people filming this scene.
14   The butler would really like to dance with the maid.
15   This is a picture about rich and poor people.
16   These people appear in other Vettriano pictures so this is not them parting forever.
17   Its title tells us the most important person in the picture.

THINKING TOGETHER

Draw an empty beach with four people. What are they doing? If they are working or playing, what jobs are they doing or what game might they be playing? Make up a storyboard to show what happened before and after your picture.

TALKING POINTS: *FARBSTUDIE QUADRATE* BY WASSILY KANDINSKI

(To see this artwork, search Google Images for *Farbstudie Quadrate*.)

Talking Points

Kandinski was a Russian painter who was the first artist to create abstract paintings. Look carefully at Kandinski's picture of twelve coloured squares with circles. Think about these ideas and talk together to decide on a group response. What are your opinions and what are your reasons for these ideas?

1   Kandinski could not paint people so he just stuck to shapes.
2   Each of us sees this picture differently.
3   We can think of life in colour and detail, or just in colour.
4   He decided to leave out any detail and simply paint the colours in simple shapes.
5   Yellow is trumpets; we can match other colours with other musical instruments.
6   We can think of some music that would go well with this picture.
7   This artwork would be just the same upside down or on its side.
8   Looking at colour can make you feel better, or at least different.
9   In the picture, yellow seems to move towards us, and blue seems to move away.
10   Red is warmth and purple is cooled red.
11   Circles are symmetrical and have a magical property.
12   The way we see each circle depends on its colours.
13   We can say which circle appeals to us most and why.
14   A curved line is a mix of horizontal and vertical forces.
15   This is a dramatic picture.

THINKING TOGETHER

Work together to create your own version of this picture. What will you use – paint or collage? What colours will you use and why? Can you create a version of this picture on the computer? Evaluate your picture and think of other ways you might use shape and colour.

TALKING POINTS: ALL THE CHILDREN OF THE WORLD

More than nine million children die every year before they reach their fifth birthday. Some reasons for many of these unnecessary deaths are poverty, illness and war.

1 Research: look at the websites listed below

Find out about children's lives and some of the ways people have tried to help the most vulnerable children. Think with your group. Try to decide which aspect of children's lives around the world would be your favourite starting point for finding out more.

2 Discuss these Talking Points

- We are lucky to be living where we do.
- The problems are too big; we cannot help all these other children.
- Charities just want money and we cannot raise enough.
- There are things that we think we might be able to do.
- It is important to try to help others not as fortunate as ourselves.
- It is important to know about what happens to other children.
- We can agree on a particular place or group of children who need our help.

THINKING TOGETHER

The United Nations estimate there to be 100 million street children worldwide. Street children in Guatemala have a life expectancy of around four years on the street. What does your group think about this?

Websites: All the children of the world

Fairtrade Schools
What we buy to wear and eat makes a difference
www.fairtrade.org.uk/schools

World of Children
Give up your birthday to help others?
www.worldofchildren.org

Sleeping Children around the World
What sort of help is a blanket?
www.scaw.org

Save the Children Fund
'Every child is born to shine'
www.savethechildren.org.uk

SOS Children
Matching orphaned children with a new family
www.soschildrensvillages.org.uk

Action for Children
Supporting needy children in the UK
www.actionforchildren.org.uk

Barnardos
Bringing out the best in every child
www.barnardos.org.uk

Great Ormond Street Hospital
Caring for very ill children: 'Keep the Magic Alive'
www.gosh.org

Abaana
A charity for the children of Africa (19,000 children die each day in Africa)
www.abaana.org

Plan International
Changing the world one child at a time
http://plan-international.org

Street children
Where do they come from?
www.toybox.org.uk

Talking Points
for poems and stories

These Talking Points are not generally to do with analysis of the technical aspects of language, but ask children to reflect on the words and ideas that make up the poem. The lists of Talking Points are long, so that there is always plenty to discuss. You might want to use just a few of the points initially, or see how the groups respond to choosing their own talk topic from the list.

Group talk about opinions and ideas such as this takes time; and the plenary sharing of ideas takes more time. As you know, this has some important implications for planning.

Further work based on the discussion can be individual, pair or group work. Outcomes include compiling a dialogue; a story; a display; a description or explanation of ideas; an analysis of the poem or of the discussion; work based on the final Thinking Together idea, which concludes each Talking Points resource; research about the author; a role play, hot seat or other drama using the ideas raised by the group; or writing a poem.

Each Talking Points session could be concluded by asking individual children some further questions:

- How would you summarise your response to this poem?
- Is it interesting and worth discussing?
- Did the discussion help you to see more in it?
- How can we 'capture' the ideas raised by the discussion?
- What other poem or story can you suggest for discussion?
- What other poem or story can you provide Talking Points for?

Children can be asked to take the poem home for further discussion with family and friends. The text of some poems (such as *The Pied Piper of Hamelin*) is too long for inclusion here but I trust classic works like this are readily available to you. Finally, no doubt you will have your own favourite poems that you and your class can write Talking Points for.

IN THE STATION OF THE METRO
BY EZRA POUND

> The apparition of these faces in the crowd;
>
> Petals on a wet, black bough.

Talking Points

1   'Apparition' – we can think of some meanings of this word.

2   The station was very busy.

3   The writer liked what he saw.

4   He could have been in any city with a metro – Tyne and Wear, Manchester, Paris, San Francisco, Leeds, Adelaide – and seen the same sort of crowds.

5   The writer was alone.

6   He was waiting at the station for someone he knew.

7   No one spoke to him.

8   'Petals on a wet, black bough' sounds like a Japanese picture.

9   The poem is a kind of haiku.

10   The poem does not contain any verbs – this makes a difference.

11   Both lines are equally important.

Talking Points—continued

12 The black bough is dark and foreboding; the petals are cherry blossom.

13 This poem is about good things that come out of bad situations.

14 The poem is not about anything; it is just a picture.

15 The poem is an instant of human thought, not really a real situation.

16 The semi-colon could be erased.

Note: Metro is short for metropolitan, and is used as a name for transport systems in many cities of the world. **Ezra Pound** was an American who lived in London, France and Italy. This poem was inspired by arriving at La Concorde station on the Paris metro in 1912. It took a year to write.

THINKING TOGETHER

Where have you been in a crowd of people?

Think together to write a poem of no more than fourteen words describing how you think people appear when they are in a crowd.

FLANKING SHEEP IN MOSEDALE
BY DAVID SCOTT

All summer the sheep were strewn like crumbs

across the fell, until the bracken turned brittle

and it was time they were gathered

into the green patchwork of closer fields.

Dogs and men sweep a whole hillside in minutes

save for the stray, scared into a scramble

up a gully. A dog is detached: whistled off

by the shepherd, who in one hand

holds a pup straining at the baling twine

and in the other a crook, light as a baton.

His call cuts the wind across the tarn:

it is the voice of the first man who

booted it across this patch to bring

strays to the place where he would have them.

You can tell that here is neither love nor money

but the old game fathers have taught sons to win.

You can see it is done well, when the dogs

lie panting, and the sheep encircled dare not move.

Talking Points

1   It is a cold autumn afternoon in the Lake District.

2   The writer regularly walks on the fells.

3   We can describe the dogs.

4   By 'detached' the writer means 'separated'.

5   The puppy is a nuisance and should have been left at the farm.

6   The sheep are very weak and rather silly creatures.

7   The men are in total control of the dogs and sheep.

8   Rounding up sheep is not particularly difficult.

9   The men are thinking about being somewhere warmer.

10   They have no real interest in the sheep except as a kind of cash crop.

11   A man can communicate with his dog in several ways.

12   The man who whistles has inherited the skill of controlling a dog.

13   These men are simply doing a job that they know how to do.

14   People have always wanted to control their environment.

15   The writer does not speak to the men, but admires them immensely.

Vocabulary

Mosedale: a valley in the Lake District. Mosedale Beck runs into Wastwater.

beck: stream

fell: mountain

gully: small high valley created by water erosion

baling twine: robust string used to bind straw bales

tarn: mountain lake

HIGH FLIGHT (AN AIRMAN'S ECSTASY) BY JOHN GILLESPIE MAGEE

Oh, I have slipped the surly bonds of earth

And fled the sky on laughter-silvered wings;

Sunwards I've climbed and joined the tumbling

    mirth

Of sun-split clouds – and done a hundred things

You have not dreamed of: wheeled and soared and

    swung

High in the sun-lit silence. Hovering there

I've chased the shouting wind along, and flung

My eager craft through footless halls of air. . .

Up, up the long, delirious, burning blue

I've topped the wind-swept heights with easy

    grace,

Where never lark, or ever eagle flew;

And while, with silent lifting mind I've trod

The high untrespassed sanctity of space,

Put out my hand, and touched the face of God.

Talking Points

1   The airman loves flying alone.

2   There seems to be no *sound* in the poem, apart from the wind.

3   There are several words to do with *light* and *happiness*.

4   The airman feels superior to people on the ground.

5   At 19 years old, he was not old enough to be flying alone like this.

6   He flies his plane in a dangerous way to show off.

7   The Spitfire reached heights that were unusual in the 1940s.

8   The airman found that height and speed gave him freedom.

9   It was summer.

10 Earth is 'surly' and space a 'sanctity' – this is not sensible thinking.

11 The poem is a kind of hymn.

12 The airman had some idea that he might die as part of his job.

13 He is not writing about fear.

14 The poem is a good tribute to any aircraft pilot.

Note: John Gillespie Magee was an American who trained as a pilot in England during the Second World War. Aged 19, he flew Spitfires (single-seater fighter planes) in combat over France and Germany. He wrote this poem and sent it to his parents just after testing a new aircraft. Three months later, he died in a crash with another plane over Lincolnshire.

BRUCE ISMAY'S SOLILOQUY
BY DEREK MAHON

They say I got away in a boat
And humbled me at the enquiry. I tell you
I sank as far that night as any
Hero. As I sat shivering in the dark water
I turned to ice to hear my costly
Life go thundering down in a pandemonium of
Prams, pianos, sideboards, winches,
Boilers bursting and shredded ragtime. Now I hide
In a lonely house behind the sea
Where the tide leaves broken toys and hatboxes
Silently at my door. The showers of
April, flowers of May mean nothing to me, nor the
Late light of June, when my gardener
Describes to strangers how the old man stays
        in bed
On seaward mornings after nights of
Wind, and will see no one, repeat no one. Then
        it is
I drown again with all those dim
Lost faces I never understood. My poor soul
Screams out in the starlight, heart
Breaks loose and rolls down like a stone.
Include me in your lamentations.

Note: Bruce Ismay was Chairman of the White Star Line that owned the Titanic. He and 2,222 other people were on the ship on its maiden voyage in April 1912. During the ship's design stage, Ismay had reduced the numbers of lifeboats she carried, to make room for luxurious cabins and restaurants. When the ship hit an iceberg and sank, he was one of the 706 survivors. This is the telegram he sent from the rescue ship Carpathia to the New York office of the White Star Line:

```
Date: 17th April 1912 Origin: Carpathia Sent: 5.50am
To:    Islefrank New York
Deeply regret advise you Titanic sunk this morning fifteenth
after collision iceberg resulting serious loss life further
particulars later.
```

Talking Points

1 'They' were right!

2 Ismay cannot forget every detail of the night the boat sank.

3 The loss of the beautiful ship affected him more than the loss of life.

4 The captain and the musicians stayed aboard; Ismay should have too.

5 Ismay suggests that he is some sort of hero.

6 The sinking of the Titanic ended his career and that is why he is depressed.

7 He was so rich that he never considered poorer people.

8 Ismay was completely responsible for the people on board the Titanic.

9 When the iceberg struck, he put himself first.

10 He had no chance to give up his place on the lifeboat.

11 He didn't think the ship would sink; now he wishes he had drowned.

12 He is right to feel dreadful.

13 Toys and hatboxes say to Ismay, 'women and children first'!

14 Living 'behind the sea' does not allow him to hide.

15 He is trying to give an account of himself that will make people kinder to him.

16 Living near the sea in his old age is a bad idea.

17 He is still rich and comfortable despite his huge mistakes.

18 He does not think he is to blame despite his wrong decisions about the lifeboats.

19 He can never be forgiven – because of course he is unforgivable.

20 He blames the disaster for his unhappiness.

21 Ismay is just sorry for himself and wants us to be sorry for him.

THE DOOR
BY RICHARD EDWARDS

A white door in a hawthorn hedge

Who lives through there?

A sorcerer? A wicked witch

With serpents in her hair?

A king enchanted into stone?

A lost princess?

A servant girl who works all night

Spinning a cobweb dress?

A queen with slippers made of ice?

I'd love to see.

A white door in a hawthorn hedge –

I wish I had a key.

Talking Points

1   Hawthorn blossom is white. The 'door' is really just the tree's flowers, and the poet imagines there is a door.

2   It is a nice afternoon in the summer holidays.

3   All the people in the poem come from story books – we can say which, for at least some of them . . .

4   The writer is imagining things.

5   The door looks like a front door, or a castle door, or a back door, or . . .

6   Looking at the last two lines – the 'key' to the door is imagination, so the writer does have the key.

7   We can write an extra verse, using characters from books we have read.

Vocabulary

sorcerer: magician

serpents: snakes

slippers: delicate shoes

THINKING TOGETHER

Draw a picture from inside the door, looking out at what is going on. Label the picture with as much detail as you can. Think together to make up a short poem from the point of view of one of the people going by.

THE INVISIBLE BEAST
BY JACK PRELUTSKY

The beast that is invisible

Is stalking through the park,

But you cannot see it coming

Though it isn't very dark.

Oh you know it's out there somewhere

Though just why you cannot tell,

But although you cannot see it

It can see you very well. . .

Oh your heart is beating faster,

Beating louder than a drum,

For you hear its footsteps falling

And your body's frozen numb.

And you cannot scream for terror

And your fear you cannot quell,

For although you cannot see it,

It can see you very well. . .

Talking Points

1 The beast is a large furry creature with huge paws and extremely sharp teeth.

2 This poem is set in the afternoon, outside.

3 The person in the poem has done something wrong and is afraid of the consequences.

4 The person in the poem is a girl.

5 The person in the poem is dreaming.

6 The beast is imaginary.

7 The beast stops being invisible when it catches you.

8 The beast never actually catches anyone.

9 The poem is about when you lose confidence in yourself, or feel scared or shy in a way that stops you doing things you'd really like to do.

THINKING TOGETHER

Add another verse to the poem. Write a poem from the beast's point of view. Draw and label a picture of the beast.

THE QUARREL
BY ELEANOR FARJEON

I quarrelled with my brother

I don't know what about

One thing led to another

And somehow we fell out.

The start of it was slight,

The end of it was strong,

He said he was right,

I knew he was wrong!

We hated one another.

The afternoon turned black.

Then suddenly my brother

Thumped me on the back,

And said, 'Oh *come* along!

We can't go on all night –

I was in the wrong.'

So he was in the right.

Talking Points

1 The poem is written by a boy.

2 The brother in the poem is older.

3 The brother in the poem is nice – no, he is horrible. . .

4 The writer is badly behaved and argumentative.

5 It is raining and no one can get out of the house to play.

6 It is understandable why the brother thumps the writer.

7 They often fall out.

8 We can think of times like this with brothers, sisters or friends.

9 Looking at the last two lines, we can explain why the brother is wrong *and* right.

10 The poem has a happy ending.

THINKING TOGETHER

Think together to re-write the poem from the brother's point of view, or draw the brother and sister and add speech bubbles to show what they might say to each other during the quarrel, and during the last four lines.

HELPING'S EASY
BY I. YATES

Helping's easy

I've done it stacks of times

I've helped Tim do his sums

But somehow he still

Got them wrong.

I helped Jessica catch a spider

And put it down Gary Williams' back

But Gary didn't laugh

Even though it was funny.

I helped Mandeep

Wash his mum's carpet

While she was bathing the baby

But she sent me home before we could

Clear up the water.

I offered to do a spot of cooking

In the kitchen with my mum

But she said

'I can do without your help,

Thank you!'

Talking Points

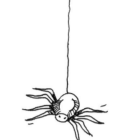

1 The writer is a girl.

2 The writer is careless and lazy.

3 The writer enjoys teasing others and messing around.

4 The writer tries to be: good; bad; helpful; a nuisance.

5 The writer really doesn't try at all. Things just happen.

6 The writer doesn't understand why things go wrong.

7 The writer has 'helped' Mum before.

8 Helping is supposed to make things easier for people, but doesn't always.

9 Tim, Gary and Mandeep are all hard to please.

10 Gary has no sense of humour.

11 Mum is ungrateful.

THINKING TOGETHER

Think together to write another verse about this person helping, or think together to draw Jessica, Mandeep and Gary and add speech bubbles to show their point of view.

WAKING AT NIGHT
BY J. KENWARD

I woke in the night

It was still as still

I thought: shall I get out of bed?

I will!

I crept to the window –

No-one there,

But a clutter of stars

In the cool night air.

I looked at the sky.

It was sprayed and split

With a hundred lights

At the heart of it.

I held my breath

And I crept . . . and crept. . .

Nobody heard me.

Everybody slept.

So I curled up, round

As a bun, in bed.

Some of the stars

Stayed in my head.

Talking Points

1 The writer has their own room.

2 It is a big house with a large family.

3 It's winter.

4 The writer isn't a person; it's a cat.

5 In verse four, we can say where the writer crept to. . .

6 Looking at the last two lines, the stars are an unpleasant memory.

7 The whole thing is just a dream.

8 The writer is glad to have seen the night sky.

9 We know what it's like to wake at night and creep about.

THINKING TOGETHER

Write an extra verse where the writer sees, or creeps up to, the moon. Write a poem from the point of view of one of the 'sleeping people', who is actually only pretending to be asleep.

SPRING POOLS
BY ROBERT FROST

These pools that, though in forests, still reflect

The total sky almost without defect,

And like the flowers beside them, chill and shiver,

Will like the flowers beside them soon be gone,

And yet not out by any brook or river,

But up by roots to bring dark foliage on.

The trees that have it in their pent-up buds

To darken nature and be summer woods –

Let them think twice before they use their powers

To blot out and drink up and sweep away

These flowery waters and these watery flowers

From snow that melted only yesterday.

Vocabulary

defect: fault

brook: stream

foliage: leaves

pent-up: shut tight

Talking Points

1   The poem is set in early spring, in a pine wood.

2   It is a still, calm day with a blue sky.

3   The flowers are white.

4   The pools *and* the flowers are both chill and shivery.

5   The flowers are growing on the ground, not on the tree.

6   The trees use their powers to do three things to the pools.

7   The trees also have an effect on the spring flowers.

8   We can add to and complete a flow diagram to show what happens to the snow:

9   The trees have no powers. They are not magic.

10   The snow has completely gone by the end of the poem.

11   Something will go wrong if the buds open too
soon – the trees should not act hastily.

12   The trees are reflected in the pools and look as if they are thinking.

13   The trees actually know best when to open their leaves.

THINKING TOGETHER

Draw and label a picture of this scene. Write a poem about this from the point of view of a squirrel.

LOVELIEST OF TREES, THE CHERRY NOW BY A.E. HOUSMAN

Loveliest of trees, the cherry now
Is hung with bloom along the bough,
And stands about the woodland ride
Wearing white for Eastertide.

Now, of my threescore years and ten,
Twenty will not come again,
And take from seventy years a score,
That only leaves me fifty more.

And since to look at things in bloom
Fifty springs are little room,
About the woodlands I will go
To see the cherry hung with snow.

Vocabulary

bough: branch

woodland ride: wide clear path through trees

threescore: sixty

score: twenty

bloom: flower or blossom

Talking Points

1   The poem is set in the woods on a fine day in spring.

2   The writer is on holiday, or at least has a day off.

3   The idea that people live 'threescore years and ten' is taken from the Bible. It is rather out of date now that we have better food and better medicine.

4   The writer is twenty years old.

5   The writer is thinking that his life is passing by too fast.

6   We can say where there is a cherry tree – or another tree that has spring blossom.

7   We can think of some other things that only happen once a year that are worth taking time to see, such as. . .

8   We could draw a picture of this scene.

9   The writer is wrong. Fifty years is plenty of time to see trees in bloom.

10   The cherry isn't really 'hung with snow'.

11   The writer sounds like a sensible person.

THINKING TOGETHER

Think together to write a poem like this about being the age you are; think about all the important things you want to do in life.

TROUT LEAPING IN THE RIVER ARUN WHERE A JUGGLER WAS DROWNED
BY CHARLES DALMAN

His flesh and bones have long since gone

But still the stream runs gaily on

And still his merry ghost contrives

To juggle with his silver knives.

Talking Points

1   The poem is too short to say anything much.

2   It is an unpleasant poem about death by drowning.

3   The writer is sorry for the juggler.

4   The poem provides a picture of jumping fish in a mountain stream.

5   It is a sort of ghost story. The fish ate the juggler.

6   The juggler was good at what he did.

7   The writer was jealous of the juggler and drowned him.

8   Half of the poem is in its title.

9   It's a warning to stop people playing with knives while swimming.

10 Trout know nothing about juggling. They always jump like that.

11 It's enjoyable because you have to think to understand it.

12 You could replace 'contrives' with a better word, which is. . .

13 It's just another reminder about water safety.

14 We do not like this poem.

15 The juggler was a miserable person, and so is the writer.

16 There was no juggler. The writer invented the whole thing.

17 It would be interesting to write a similar short poem about fish, juggling, how things appear, or a ghost story.

THINKING TOGETHER

Decide together on how you would summarise your response to this poem. Is it interesting and worth discussing? Did the discussion help you to see more in it?

TALL NETTLES
BY EDWARD THOMAS

Tall nettles cover up, as they have done

These many springs, the rusty harrow, the plough

Long worn out, and the roller made of stone.

Only the elm butt tops the nettles now.

This corner of the farmyard I like most:

As well as any bloom upon a flower

I like the dust on nettles, rarely lost

Except to prove the sweetness of a shower.

Talking Points

1 Lots of clues show that this poem was written a long time ago.

2 It provides a reminder of how farms used to be.

3 The nettles are weeds and should be destroyed.

4 The writer is a farmer who is wasting time.

5 The elm tree stump is the only thing nearby taller than the nettles.

6 The farm went out of business because of bad management.

7 The writer likes things the way they are.

8 It's unusual to prefer nettles to flowers, and rain to fine weather.

9 Nettle leaves are often dusty because they are spiny and catch dust.

10 The dust is a reminder that some things do well if left undisturbed.

11 The poem was written in June.

12 We dislike this poem.

13 The writer is taking a break while helping with the corn harvest.

14 The writer was killed in the First World War. So it's good to know he had time to look at simple things and enjoy them. But it makes you wonder how much he enjoyed being a soldier.

15 It makes you wish it was summer and we were all outside.

16 It would be interesting to write a poem that changes how people look at things they don't usually like, such as nettles, wasps, slugs, and so on.

THINKING TOGETHER

Summarise your response to this poem. Is it interesting and worth discussing? Did the discussion help you to see more in it?

THE VIXEN
BY JOHN CLARE

Among the taller wood with ivy hung

The vixen plays and dances round her young.

She snuffs and barks if any passes by

And swings her tail and turns prepared to fly.

Horse riders hurry by, she runs to see,

And turns again, from danger never free.

If any stops she runs among the poles

And barks and snaps and drives them in their holes.

They get all still and lie in safety sure

And out again when everything's secure

To jump and snap at blackbirds bouncing by

To fight and catch the great white butterfly.

Talking Points

1 The vixen lives in a den in the wood.

2 She has several young cubs that she cares for well.

3 There is a village near the wood.

4 This poem was written a long time ago. Still, some things don't change.

5 The vixen imagines dangers that are not there.

6 The cubs only come out at night. They are very wary.

7 The vixen and cubs understand each other.

8 The writer is a city person who does not understand that foxes are vermin and should be controlled by hunting.

9 The cubs are just learning how to catch their own food.

10 The poem is set in summer.

11 The poem makes the scene easy to imagine. You could almost paint it.

12 We think this poem is rather dull and tells us nothing.

13 The vixen is old and tired. She represents wildlife in general.

14 The fox cubs are safe once inside the den.

THINKING TOGETHER

Think together to draw and describe how another animal behaves in its natural surroundings – a mouse, woodlouse or grass snake, for example.

OPEN ALL THE CAGES
BY RICHARD EDWARDS

Open all the cages

Let the parrots fly –

Green and gold and purple parrots

Streaming up the sky.

Open all the cages

Let the parrots out

Screeching, squawking, parrots swooping

Happily about.

Open all the cages

Set the parrots free

Flocks of parrots flapping homewards

South across the sea.

Silent trees in silent forests

Long for parrots, so –

Open all the cages

Let the parrots go!

Talking Points

1   The writer likes animals.

2   The parrots are in cages in a zoo.

3   In the wild, parrots live safely in rainforests.

4   It would be cruel to let parrots out. Other birds would kill them.

5   If free, parrots would kill British birds such as the robin or sparrow.

6   Birds have an easy life in a cage so don't want to be let out.

7   Rainforests are being cut down so we need to keep some parrots in cages, or they might disappear altogether.

8   It's better to have animals where people can see them easily.

9   Children need to learn about wildlife, so we need zoos.

10   The word 'streaming' is good because. . .

11   Most parrots can't actually fly.

12   Parrots are big, aggressive birds that have to be kept in cages.

13   You could use the word 'ideas' instead of 'parrots'.

14   We don't like this poem because. . .

15   We like this poem because. . .

THINKING TOGETHER

Think together to write a poem about other caged animals; which would you set free? What does a lion think as he or she watches us in our cars?

SNOW
BY LOUIS MCNEICE

The room was suddenly rich and the great bay-
        window was
Spawning snow and pink roses against it
Soundlessly collateral and incompatible:
World is suddener than we fancy it.

World is crazier and more of it than we think,
Incorrigibly plural. I peel and portion
A tangerine and spit the pips and feel
The drunkenness of things being various.

And the fire flames with a bubbling sound for
        world
Is more spiteful and gay than one supposes –
On the tongue on the eyes on the ears in the
        palms of one's hands –
There is more than glass between the snow and the
        huge roses.

Vocabulary

spawning: making

collateral: accompanying or supporting

plural: many

incompatible: unable to agree

incorrigible: cannot be corrected by punishment

Talking Points

1   The cut roses seem to be dying once it starts snowing outside.

2   It takes a change of weather to alert us to ordinary things.

3   The light in the room changed because of the snow.

4   We each experience things differently.

5   The tangerine is more a taste than a colour.

6   The writer is alone.

7   The fire and the tangerine have a lot in common.

8   There are examples here of things that appeal to all our senses.

9   'Between' does not mean unity but separation.

10   The poem has an air of menace.

11   There is an artificial fire and artificial roses.

12   Sometimes you can feel happy for no reason.

13   The house is isolated, on a hill, and the snow blocks the writer in.

THINKING TOGETHER

We can write some key ideas for a poem about two things separated by a glass window – a cat and the rain, a child and the dark, a caged creature and the wild . . .

WHY BROWNLEE LEFT
BY PAUL MULDOON

Why Brownlee left, and where he went,

Is a mystery even now.

For if a man should have been content

It was him; two acres of barley,

One of potatoes, four bullocks,

A milker, a slated farmhouse.

He was last seen going out to plough

On a March morning, bright and early.

By noon Brownlee was famous;

They had found all abandoned, with

The last rig unbroken, his pair of black

Horses, like man and wife,

Shifting their weight from foot to

Foot, and gazing into the future.

Talking Points

1   The poem is set in Ireland.

2   Brownlee was a farmer who hated ploughing.

3   It was his birthday.

4   Brownlee lived alone.

5   The farm house was near a small, quiet village.

6   He ploughed up some treasure and ran away with it.

7   A neighbour was the last person to see him.

8   The horses understood why he went.

9   Brownlee was unbearably lonely, or angry, or afraid.

10   Brownlee had not thought about leaving before he did.

11   At the moment when he left, he had two possible futures.

12   The end of line 13 and the start of line 14 show the way the horses were moving.

13   His neighbours envied him, before and after he left.

14   It is sad when people leave home forever.

15   The poem answers its own title question.

GORILLA
BY MARTIN HONEYSETT

A giant gorilla came to tea

Whoever asked him? It wasn't me

He came in through the kitchen wall,

It took six chairs to seat him all.

He drank his tea straight from the pot

And sandwiches – he ate the lot.

He poked the jellies to make them wobble,

Then swallowed them up with just one gobble.

All that remained on the plate was the cake,

There was nothing else for him to take.

When he'd eaten that I showed him the door,

And hoped he'd go now there was no more.

Instead he ate the door as well,

Except for the knocker and the bell.

After that at last he decided to go,

Who invited him? I'd like to know.

Talking Points

1 The gorilla likes going to birthday parties.

2 The gorilla is looking for somewhere to live.

3 We think we are as bad as the gorilla sometimes.

4 The gorilla is made up.

5 The gorilla got out of the zoo.

6 Gorillas are actually quiet, gentle creatures.

7 We would like to invite the gorilla to tea, or to visit our class.

THINKING TOGETHER

Think together to draw the table with six chairs, the teapot, the sandwiches, the jellies and the cake on the plate. Decide what else you would like to have if a gorilla came to tea. Decide who you would invite. Make an invitation. Don't forget to think of what people should wear.

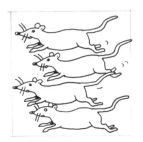

THE PIED PIPER BY ROBERT BROWNING

Make sure you have a copy of the poem to look at. Read the poem aloud. Think about these ideas. What do you think? What do others think? Use evidence from the poem to support your discussion.

The year is about 1510; Hamelin is in Germany.

Talking Points

1 The rats lived in the riverbank and in people's houses.

2 The Mayor and Corporation were very poor leaders for the city people.

3 The Pied Piper was a magician.

4 People will promise anything when they are desperate.

5 The Mayor really did mean to pay the Piper.

6 The music for the rats was high pitched and squeaky.

7 The Mayor thought the Piper was greedy.

8 The Piper needed the money to live on.

9 The Piper expected the people to be able to afford to have the rats removed.

10 Whatever the Mayor had done, it was not fair of the Piper to steal the children.

11 The children were enchanted by the music.

12 The lame boy was lucky to be left behind.

THINKING TOGETHER

Think together to make up a sentence that starts, 'The message of this poem is . . .'. Draw a banner with rats holding it up to display your sentence.

THE HIGHWAYMAN
BY ALFRED NOYES

Make sure you have a copy of the poem to look at. Read the poem aloud. Discuss these ideas. What do you think? What do others think? Use evidence from the poem to support your discussion.

Talking Points

1   The Highwayman was a thief and a criminal.

2   Bess was afraid of Tim.

3   Tim was jealous of the Highwayman.

4   The arrival of the soldiers was a coincidence.

5   Bess had no choice about what she could do, once she was tied up.

6   The soldiers were just doing their job – keeping the roads clear of robbers.

7   It was the night of the full moon.

8   Bess was brave and fearless.

9   Once he knew Bess was dead, there was no point in the Highwayman returning to the Inn.

10   The soldiers gave Tim money.

11   The Highwayman returned to the Inn to take revenge on Tim.

12   Bess's father found out what had happened, and thought of a way to punish Tim.

13   Tim was happy once the Highwayman was dead.

14   The story is not a tragedy because the Highwayman was a criminal.

15   There are no such things as ghosts.

16   Bess and the Highwayman do not live on as ghosts, but as story characters.

THINKING TOGETHER

Think together to make up a storyboard in which the soldiers do not arrive in time; the Highwayman robs a coach and shoots a lady; and Tim decides to become his apprentice. What happens?

PETER PAN
BY J.M. BARRIE

Make sure you have a copy of the story to look at. Read the story. Think about these ideas. What do you think? What do others think, and why? Can you come to an agreement in your group?

Talking Points

1 Mr and Mrs Darling were irresponsible, going out and leaving the children alone.

2 No dog can look after children.

3 Shadows cannot come unstuck from people's feet.

4 You can't keep a shadow in a drawer – it would get mixed up with other shadows.

5 The Darling children were spoilt and badly behaved.

6 Peter is very grumpy and cross all the time. He should grow up.

7 Growing up means accepting responsibility for your own actions.

8 Peter likes listening to stories.

9 Wendy is really fussy and pretends to be Peter's mother.

10 Tootles is clumsy and silly.

11 Tinker Bell is a truly evil character.

12 No Lost Boy is allowed to know anything that Peter doesn't.

13 The copyright of Peter Pan now belongs to Great Ormond Street Hospital for children, so it is important that the story keeps on being popular.

THINKING TOGETHER

Think together to draw the scene in Peter Pan where the dog Nana chases Peter and catches his shadow as he flies from the window. Annotate your drawing with your ideas about the story.

THE ONCE AND FUTURE KING
BY T.H. WHITE

**When Arthur is young, Merlin turns him into
other creatures, so that he can experience how
they live. Here, Arthur has been turned into an ant.**

The place where he was seemed like a great field of boulders, with a flattened
fortress at one end of it. The fortress was entered by tunnels in the rock, and,
over the entrance to each tunnel, there was a notice that said:

EVERYTHING NOT FORBIDDEN IS COMPULSORY

He read the notice with dislike, though he did not understand its meaning.
He thought to himself: I will explore a little, before going in. For some
reason the notice gave him a reluctance to go, making the rough tunnel look
sinister.

Then he became conscious of something that had been waiting to be
noticed – that there was a noise in his head that was articulate. It was either a
noise or a complicated smell, and the easiest way to explain it is to say that it
was like a wireless broadcast. It came through his antennae. The music had a
monotonous rhythm like a pulse, and words that went with it were about
June-moon-noon-spoon, or Mammy-mammy-mammy, or Ever-never, or
Blue-true-you. He liked them at first, especially the ones about Love-dove-
above, until he found that they did not vary. As soon as they had been
finished once, they were begun again. After an hour or two, they began to
make him feel sick inside.

(He meets another ant). The extraordinary thing was that he could not
ask questions. In order to ask them, he would have had to put them into
language through his antennae – and he now discovered, with a helpless
feeling, that there were no words for the things he wanted to say.

There were no words for happiness, for freedom, for liking, nor were there any words for their opposites. The nearest he could get to Right or Wrong, even, was to say Done or Not Done.

'What are you doing?'

The boy answered truthfully, 'I am not doing anything.'

The ant was baffled by this for several seconds, as you would be if Einstein had told you his latest ideas about space. Then it extended the twelve joints of its aerial and spoke past him into the blue.

It said: '105978/UDC reporting from square five. There is an insane ant on square five. Over to you.'

The word it used for insane was Not-Done.

Vocabulary

sinister: threatening

articulate: speaking in words that have a meaning

wireless: radio

monotonous: lacking in variety, or the same all the time

THINKING TOGETHER

Think together to adapt the sign above the ant tunnel for your classroom. What words could you use to describe what is expected of everyone?

Talking Points

Discuss these ideas, giving reasons for your opinions.

1   Arthur is afraid of the ants.

2   Merlin has put Arthur in danger.

3   Ants live in communities in which the individual is not important.

4   The notice over the door is not sinister but just making sure everyone sticks to the rules.

5   The noise in his head was coming from all the other ants.

6   The words in our minds are only our own thoughts, not those of others.

7   Words are essential for asking questions.

8   Without language each of us would be helpless.

9   There are other ways of communicating, without words.

10   The ant could not think for itself.

11   'Not-Done' is forbidden and 'Done' is compulsory.

12   We can say these sentences in ant language:

  - The blue-true-you music is interesting.
  - Our leader is wonderful.
  - The other ant colony is our enemy.
  - A new find of seeds for food is brilliant.
  - Falling off the nest is dangerous.
  - Being stepped on is a disaster.

13   Arthur would be sorry to leave the ant colony.

14   The ant leader is different from all the other ants.

15   People never behave like ants.

117

Talking Points
for lists

Talking Points Lists are designed to stimulate and sustain wide-ranging discussion. They focus on enabling children to articulate their own ideas and listen to the ideas of others. In essence, children working with others in talk groups are asked to decide whether they think particular items should be **included** in a particular list of items – and why, or why not. Children then talk together to add their own ideas to the list.

Discussion involves children suggesting ideas and offering reasons for what they say, then deciding on a group answer. There are no right or wrong answers. But there are more or less sensible reasons, which can be expressed and considered through talk.

It is important that children take the time to ask all members of their group for their ideas before coming to a decision. Groups should be aware that their reasoning is a key part of their work together, and that they will be asked to explain how their group has negotiated and agreed list items to the class.

BENEFITS OF DISCUSSION OF TALKING POINTS LISTS

- an inclusive, open activity to help children share ideas;
- talk fosters children's individual imagination and creativity;
- little reading and writing are required;
- children can articulate their ideas in the 'safe' forum of a peer discussion group;
- no answer is right or wrong, but ideas may be more interesting or unusual or perceptive;
- examples of reasoning can be shared;
- children learn and practice how to think aloud together;
- the discussion is motivated by children's own ideas;
- it is an opportunity for exploratory talk;
- further work; for example, research, writing, or drama, can be based on group talk.

TALKING POINTS LIST 1: THINGS THAT ARE A WASTE OF TIME

Talking Points

Think aloud together. Read the title of the list. Think about the items on the list; would you agree that they should be included in the list, or not? What are your reasons?

- walking a dog
- going to a shopping centre
- washing up
- playing a computer game
- writing a letter
- making a cake
- any sort of gardening but especially raking leaves
- cleaning a car
- having a shower every day
- visiting relatives
- learning spellings
- sitting still
- watching the news on the television
- finding out about all the settings on a new camera or mobile phone
- tidying your room

THINKING TOGETHER

Talk together to think of three more things for this list.

TALKING POINTS LIST 2: THINGS THAT ARE ALWAYS ENJOYABLE

Talking Points

Think aloud together. Read the title of the list. Think about the items on the list; would you agree that they should be included in the list, or not? What are your reasons?

- eating ice cream
- going to the beach
- swimming
- being outside
- playing with friends
- visiting a theme park
- watching animals in the wildlife park
- making a cup of tea for someone
- going to a supermarket to choose food
- snow
- pets
- having a sleep-over
- your birthday
- a fizzy drink with ice cubes and a straw
- when someone gives you a present
- finding something you thought you'd lost

THINKING TOGETHER

Talk together to think of three more things for this list.

121

TALKING POINTS LIST 3: THINGS THAT WE WOULD LIKE TO CHANGE

Talking Points

Think aloud together. Read the title of the list. Think about the items on the list; would you agree that they should be included in the list, or not? What are your reasons?

- attending school every weekday

- the ban on eating sweets in school

- the way it is illegal for children to earn money

- the way some people behave

- how much help we get in class

- how difficult maths is

- having to do tests and exams

- what we wear to school

- the lack of time at school to do science, art or music

- the way other people decide what we learn, and when

- the way some children in the world do not have food or water

- the places we go to on holiday

- the toys or computer games we have

- cars: there should be limits on how much driving people can do

- advertising on television

- being rich or poor: everyone should have the same amount of money

THINKING TOGETHER

Talk together to think of three more things for this list.

TALKING POINTS LIST 4: THINGS THAT WE WOULD LIKE TO KEEP THE SAME

Talking Points

Think aloud together. Read the title of the list. Think about the items on the list; would you agree that they should be included in the list, or not? What are your reasons?

- the season and the weather

- the chances we get to play during a school day

- the toys and games we have to play with at school or at home

- our brothers and sisters

- our pets

- the recipe for our favourite meals

- our friends

- the chances we have to take a break during the day

- lunch

- the time we have to get up and go to bed

- the amount of pocket money we are given

- time to read

- time to do sport

- what happens during the school holidays

- the way things are at weekends

THINKING TOGETHER

Talk together to think of three more things for this list.

TALKING POINTS LIST 5: THINGS THAT SHOULD BE ROUND

Talking Points

Think aloud together. Read the title of the list. Think about the items on the list; would you agree that they should be included in the list, or not? What are your reasons?

- all coins

- a circus ring

- an apple

- the way you stir cake mix

- trunks of trees

- hoops, footballs and tennis balls

- groups of people talking

- a walk – so that you never go the same place twice

- a dome, an umbrella, or a protractor should be half round

- bubbles

- a circle you have drawn with a pair of compasses

- the sun and the moon

- the holes a hole-punch makes

- when you sing 'London Bridge is Falling Down' with a group

- a neutron star

- a dinner plate

- a ring

- the way a skipping rope turns

- the buttons on a phone

- a rain drop just before it hits the ground

- zero

THINKING TOGETHER

Talk together to think of three more things for this list.

TALKING POINTS LIST 6: THINGS TO THINK OF WHEN LYING AWAKE IN THE MIDDLE OF THE NIGHT

Talking Points

Think aloud together. Read the title of the list. Think about the items on the list; would you agree that they should be included in the list, or not? What are your reasons?

- the plot of a good story book or a film
- the most scary thing you have ever seen
- the way people look after each other
- the way people can be unkind
- plans for the next day
- memories
- music or songs
- the seven times table
- everything you have ever done wrong and now regret
- everything you have ever done right but nobody noticed
- how to get revenge
- a poem that you have learned
- something you plan to make or finish or do
- how to make someone like you
- the sounds you can hear
- the way your toes feel
- how to thank someone or give someone a treat

THINKING TOGETHER

Talk together to think of three more things for this list.

TALKING POINTS LIST 7: THINGS THAT ARE DEFINITELY GOING TO GO WRONG IN THE FUTURE

Talking Points

Think aloud together. Read the title of the list. Think about the items on the list; would you agree that they should be included in the list, or not? What are your reasons?

- Climate change will create massive problems such as flooding.

- Everyone will lose their jobs and be very poor.

- The sun will burn out and stop shining.

- There will be a plague of flies and we will all get horrible germs.

- Supermarkets will run out of food.

- The water supply will get polluted.

- There will not be a chance to choose which secondary school to go to.

- Electricity will be cut off and weekends will be long and very boring.

- All the trees will be chopped down and the land built over.

- There will be roads everywhere and nowhere to walk.

- The sea will be too dangerous to swim in.

- Life is going to be more like a computer game – fast and aggressive.

- You will not be allowed to choose what you do or say.

- Friends will move away.

THINKING TOGETHER

Talk together to think of three more things for this list.

TALKING POINTS LIST 8: THINGS ABOUT BEING AN ADULT THAT ARE BETTER THAN BEING A CHILD

Talking Points

Think aloud together. Read the title of the list. Think about the items on the list; would you agree that they should be included in the list, or not? What are your reasons?

- You can get rich.

- You can do what you like.

- You can drive a car.

- You can choose what to do in the evenings.

- You can make rules and tell other people what to do.

- You can win arguments by saying, 'Because I say so'.

- You get bigger meals.

- You can go out in the dark on your own.

- You can drink alcohol.

- You can do an interesting job.

- You can decide on the sort of holiday that will suit you.

- You can spend a lot of time and money on your hobby.

- You can have a lot of friends.

- You can have whatever pets you like.

THINKING TOGETHER

Talk together to think of three more things for this list.

127

TALKING POINTS LIST 10: THINGS THAT WE AIM TO DO IN THE FUTURE

Think aloud together. Read the title of the list. Make sure everyone in turn gets the chance to talk through their ideas. Ask some questions to find out more. Think about the items on the list; would you agree that they should be included in the list, or not? What are your reasons?

- Have a big dog, or even two – or have lots of cats.

- Grow food for the family.

- Be in the Guinness Book of Records for. . . *(think of a record you could set)*.

- Travel to Australia or America.

- Do some work for a particular charity. . . *(name it)*.

- Climb mountains. . . *(say which)*.

- Go on a long sea trip. . . *(say what sort of boat and where to)*.

- Read all the books by. . . *(name your own author)*.

- Join a band or orchestra and record music. . . *(say what sort of music)*.

- Break a record. . . *(think what sport or activity)*.

- Make up a computer game about. . .

- Go to University to study. . . *(you choose)*.

- Live in. . . *(say what sort of house, where and why)*.

- Write a best-selling book about. . .

- Be given a. . . *(think of a present you would like)*.

- Give someone. . . *(think of someone and a present you would like to give them)*.

- Make a. . . *(think what you want to make, build or invent)*.

THINKING TOGETHER

Talk together to think of three more things for this list.

Talking Points
for mathematics

Mathematical understanding involves looking for pattern and structure, and using number facts to calculate and deduce solutions. The world seems to divide into those who find mathematics simple and absorbing, and those who do not. Our overall aims for educating the children in our classrooms are to provide them with insight into mathematical thinking, to make numeracy accessible, and to enable every child to feel that they can speak the language of mathematics.

There may be no shortcuts to learning the number facts that are the basis of mathematical thinking. Individual or group tuition and games, repetition, reinforcement, and chances to put new knowledge to good use all provide children with opportunities to develop and consolidate their understanding of numbers.

Talking Points can provide a focus for discussion of factual information and tentative ideas. The talk can help children to find out what others think, and why. The examples here show the sort of ideas that can encourage children to talk about numbers, patterns and shapes. It is useful to ask groups to draw a diagram or otherwise make a note of their thinking as they go along, for later reference. Some of the Talking Points are 'correct' in mathematical terms. The discussion then focuses on how the group can explain the idea to one another – and the class.

TALKING POINTS: 2D AND 3D SHAPES

Talking Points

Think together to decide together whether these ideas are true or false – or if you are unsure. Discuss everyone's suggestions. Draw an example that shows what you think.

1   If the angles of a triangle are all equal, the sides all have to be equal too.

2   We can name a quadrilateral that has no parallel sides.

3   A rhombus is a squashed square.

4   Irregular polygons have sides of different lengths.

5   A cube has six faces (sides), six edges and six vertices (corners).

6   There is more than one 3D shape that has no edges or vertices.

7   We can fold a piece of paper to make a pentagon.

8   There is a 3D shape that fits this description: five flat surfaces, one of them a square. We can say what shape the other four faces are.

9   The word 'straight' is the opposite of the word 'curved'.

10   A degree is a unit that measures angle.

11   The perimeter of a hexagon is equal to six times the radius of the circumscribed circle.

12   A traffic cone, a fir-tree cone and an ice cream cone all have some things in common with a volcanic cone.

13   A triangular prism has a triangle cross-section any way you cut it.

14   This net will make a triangular prism (*see diagram on right*).

15   The plural of vertex is vertixes.

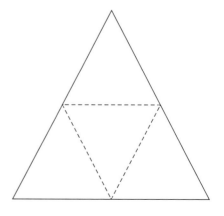

TALKING POINTS: ABOUT THE NUMBER 3

Talking Points

These Talking Points are facts about the number 3. Talk together to write or draw examples that will show your understanding of these facts about the number 3.

- 3 is the first odd prime number.

- 3 can be multiplied by 4 to make 12.

- The number 3 has three horizontal lines.

- 3 squared is 9.

- A tetrahedron has four triangular faces, three of which meet at each vertex.

- An equilateral triangle has sides of the same length.

- A number is divisible by three if the sum of its digits is divisible by three.

- Divide 3 by 6 and you get a half.

- We see light as a mix of three colours – red, blue and green.

- We hear because of three bones in the ear.

- Earth is the third planet in the solar system.

- 'Third time lucky' is just a superstition.

- 3 cubed is a number between 20 and 30.

- We can give a value of pi to three decimal places.

- In stories, things come in threes – wishes, blind mice, musketeers and bears.

- Three dimensions are needed to make a solid object.

- 100 divided by 3 = 33.333333. . .

THINKING TOGETHER

With your group, think about and research more facts about the number 3.

TALKING POINTS: ABOUT THE NUMBER 5

Talking Points

These Talking Points are facts about the number 5. Talk together to write or draw examples that will show your understanding of these facts about the number 5.

■ On phones or computers, the 5 key has a raised dot or bar so it can be found by touch.

■ 5 squared is 25.

■ *Penta* is Greek for 5 while *quinque* is Latin for 5.

■ A five-sided shape is a pentagon.

■ A starfish is a pentagram or 5-pointed star.

■ The symbol for the Olympic games is five interlocked rings; their colours represent the colours in the flags of competing countries.

■ The fifth in a series of things is four after the first.

■ $5\frac{1}{3}$ is a mixed number.

■ The mammalian design is to have pentadactyl limbs with five fingers.

■ A fifth of a hundred is twenty.

■ If travelling at 60 miles per hour, in 5 minutes you will travel 5 miles.

■ Jupiter is the fifth planet from the sun.

■ Musical notation uses a staff of five lines.

■ A quincunx is the pattern of five dots on dice, playing cards or dominoes.

■ 5 is the fifth Fibonacci number, being 2 plus 3.

THINKING TOGETHER

With your group, think about and research more facts about the number 5.

TALKING POINTS: PRIME NUMBERS

Talking Points

These Talking Points are all facts about prime numbers. Discuss them to make sure that your group can explain why they are true. Draw diagrams or make up examples to show your thinking to each other.

The prime numbers up to 100 are:

2 3 5 7 11 13 17 19 23 29 31 37 41 43 47 53 59

61 67 71 73 79 83 89 97

■ A definition of a prime number is that it has two divisors: **1** and **itself**.

■ 1 is not a prime number because it does not fit the definition.

■ The smallest 25 prime numbers are all under 100.

■ The only even prime number is 2.

■ Any even number larger than the number 2 is the sum of two primes.

■ A factor is a whole number that divides exactly into a whole number, leaving no remainder.

■ Prime numbers have two factors.

■ Prime factors are the prime numbers that can be multiplied together to make a given number.

■ We can say what the prime factors of the number 36 are.

■ There is no pattern to prime numbers on the 100 square.

■ We can find the prime numbers between 100 and 500.

Extension

Identifying prime numbers
http://en.wikipedia.org/wiki/File:Animation_Sieve_of_Eratosth-2.gif

The first 500 prime numbers
http://en.wikipedia.org/wiki/List_of_prime_numbers

TALKING POINTS: CIRCLES

Talking Points

The Talking Points here are all facts. Discuss them to make sure that your group can explain WHY they are true.

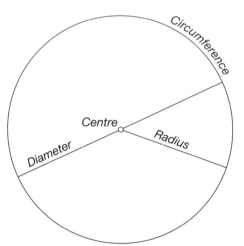

- A circle is a plane shape.

- A degree is a measure of rotation or turn. There are 360 degrees in the centre of a circle.

- The diameter is the largest distance between any two points on a circle.

- The diameter of a circle is twice the radius.

- Circumference is a special name for the perimeter of a circle.

- The circumference of a circle is just over three times the diameter.

- The ratio of the circumference to the diameter is approximately 3.141592654; we abbreviate this constant number (pi or π) to 3.142.

- You can calculate pi by dividing the circumference of a circle by its diameter.

- An arc is a section of the circumference.

- There are many examples of circles in nature and in architecture – we can give some.

- You can be inside, outside, or on a circle.

Extension

More about circles: http://windowseat.ca/circles

THINKING TOGETHER

Use drawing compasses to draw circle patterns. Draw three circles – radius 4, 6 and 8 cm. Use string to measure the circumference of each. Is it true that the value of pi is nearly 3?

TALKING POINTS: PROBABILITY

Talking Points

Think together to share all your ideas about probability.

1   Probability is about chance. We can list three things that are:

   ■ definitely going to happen

   ■ likely to happen

   ■ equally likely to happen or not happen

   ■ unlikely to happen

   ■ definitely not going to happen – impossible.

2   Use cards, dice, coins, or bags of cubes to show that you and your group can explain these ideas:

   (a)   When tossing a coin, there is an even chance of getting heads or tails. Or, a ½ chance of getting heads, ½ chance of tails.

   (b)   When throwing a dice, you have a ⅙ chance of throwing a 6. And, you have a ⅚ chance of **not** throwing a 4.

   (c)   Probability of events has to total 1. For example, if the probability of getting something is ⅓, the chance of not getting it is ⅔: ⅓ + ⅔ = 1. Show this using a bag of cubes.

3   Calculating probability means looking at how many alternatives there are, and working out the chance of you getting a particular choice.

THINKING TOGETHER

Cubes problem

In a bag, there are green and yellow cubes. All are the same size.

The probability of pulling out a yellow cube is ⅕. What is the probability of pulling out a green cube?

If there are ten cubes in the bag, how many are yellow? How many are green?

Further reading

Dawes, L. (2010) *Creating a Speaking and Listening Classroom: Integrating Talk for Learning at Key Stage 2*. London: Routledge.

Dawes, L. (2010) 'Organising Effective Classroom Talk'. In J. Arthur and T. Cremin (eds) *Learning to Teach in the Primary School*. London: Routledge (2nd Edition).

Dawes, L. (2008) *The Essential Speaking and Listening: Talk for Learning at Key Stage 2*. London: Routledge.

Dawes, L. (2008) 'Encouraging students' contributions to dialogue during science'. *School Science Review*, December 2008, 90(331), pp. 101–7.

Grugeon, E., Hubbard, L., Smith, C. and Dawes, L. (1998) *Teaching Speaking and Listening in the Primary School*. London: Fulton Press.

Loxley, P., Dawes, L., Nicholls, L. and Dore, B. (2010) *Teaching Primary Science: Promoting Enjoyment and Developing Understanding*. London: Pearson Education.

Mercer, N. (2000) *Words and Minds*. London: Routledge.

Mercer, N. and Littleton, K. (2007). *Dialogue and the Development of Children's Thinking: A Sociocultural Approach*. London: Routledge.

Mercer, N. and Hodgkinson, S. (2008) (eds) *Exploring Talk in School*. London: Sage.

Naylor, S. and Keogh, B. (2000) *Concept Cartoons in Science Education*. London: Millgate House Publishers.

Key reference for science Talking Points

Warwick, P. (2000) 'Light and Dark'. *Primary Science Review*, 64, pp. 23–5.

Thinking Together website

Our website includes downloadable materials for teaching and learning, including more examples of Talking Points. We also provide the research behind the Thinking Together approach.: http://thinkingtogether.educ.cam.ac.uk